LEON TROTSKY

LEON TROTSKY

Hedda Garza

1986
CHELSEA HOUSE PUBLISHERS
NEW YORK
NEW HAVEN   PHILADELPHIA

SENIOR EDITOR: William P. Hansen
ASSOCIATE EDITORS: John Haney
              Richard Mandell
              Marian W. Taylor
EDITORIAL COORDINATOR: Karyn Gullen Browne
EDITORIAL STAFF: Pierre Hauser
              Perry Scott King
              Alma Rodriguez-Sokol
              John Selfridge
              Bert Yaeger
ART DIRECTOR: Susan Lusk
LAYOUT: Irene Friedman
ART ASSISTANTS: Noreen Lamb
              Carol McDougall
              Victoria Tomaselli
COVER DESIGN: Carol McDougall
PICTURE RESEARCH: Matthew Miller
              Nikolai Ourousoff
              Susan Quist

First Printing

Library of Congress Cataloging in Publication Data

Garza, Hedda. LEON TROTSKY

    (World leaders past & present)
    Bibliography: p.
    Includes index.
    1. Trotsky, Leon, 1879–1940—Juvenile literature.
2. Revolutionists—Soviet Union—Biography—Juvenile
literature.   3. Statesmen—Soviet Union—Biography—
Juvenile literature.   4. Communism—Soviet Union—
Juvenile literature.   [1. Trotsky, Leon, 1879–1940.
2. Statesmen.   3. Communism—Soviet Union] I. Title.
II. Series.
DK254.T6G37   1986   947.084′092′4 [B] 92] 85—28043

ISBN 0-87754-444-1

Chelsea House Publishers
Harold Steinberg, Chairman & Publisher
Susan Lusk, Vice President
A Division of Chelsea House Educational Communications, Inc.

133 Christopher Street, New York, NY 10014

345 Whitney Avenue, New Haven, CT 06510

5014 West Chester Pike, Edgemont, PA 19028

Photos courtesy of AP/Wide World Photos, Art Resource, The Bettmann
Archive, The Tamiment Library (New York University), UPI/Bettmann
Newsphotos

Contents

ON LEADERSHIP
Arthur M. Schlesinger, jr.

LEADERSHIP, it may be said, is really what makes the world go round. Love no doubt smooths the passage; but love is a private transaction between consenting adults. Leadership is a public transaction with history. The idea of leadership affirms the capacity of individuals to move, inspire and mobilize masses of people so that they act together in pursuit of an end. Sometimes leadership serves good purposes, sometimes bad; but whether the end is benign or evil, great leaders are those men and women who leave their personal stamp on history.

Now, the very concept of leadership implies the proposition that individuals can make a difference. This proposition has never been universally accepted. From classical times to the present day, eminent thinkers have regarded individuals as no more than the agents and pawns of larger forces, whether the gods and goddesses of the ancient world or, in the modern era, race, class, nation, the dialectic, the will of the people, the spirit of the times, history itself. Against such forces, the individual dwindles into insignificance.

So contends the thesis of historical determinism. Tolstoy's great novel *War and Peace* offers a famous statement of the case. Why, Tolstoy asked, did millions of men in the Napoleonic wars, denying their human feelings and their common sense, move back and forth across Europe slaughtering their fellows? "The war," Tolstoy answered, "was bound to happen simply because it was bound to happen." All prior history predetermined it. As for leaders, they, Tolstoy said, "are but the labels that serve to give a name to an end and, like labels, they have the least possible connection with the event." The greater the leader, "the more conspicuous the inevitability and the predestination of every act he commits." The leader, said Tolstoy, is "the slave of history."

Determinism takes many forms. Marxism is the determinism of class, Nazism the determinism of race. But the idea of men and women as the slaves of history runs athwart the deepest human instincts. Rigid determinism abolishes the idea of human freedom—the assumption of free choice that underlies every move we make, every word we speak, every thought we think. It abolishes the idea of human responsibility, since it is manifestly unfair to reward or punish people for actions that are by definition beyond their control. No one can live consistently by any deterministic creed. The Marxist states prove this themselves by their extreme susceptibility to the cult of leadership.

More than that, history refutes the idea that individuals make no difference. In December 1931 a British politician crossing Park Avenue in New York City between 76th and 77th Streets around ten-thirty at night looked in the wrong direction and was knocked down by an automobile—a moment, he later recalled, of a man aghast, a world aglare: "I do not understand why I was not broken like an eggshell or squashed like a gooseberry." Fourteen months later an American politician, sitting in an open car in Miami, Florida, was fired on by an assassin; the man beside him was hit. Those who believe that individuals make no difference to history might well ponder whether the next two decades would have been the same had Mario Contasini's car killed Winston Churchill in 1931 and Giuseppe Zangara's bullet killed Franklin Roosevelt in 1933. Suppose, in addition, that Adolf Hitler had been killed in the street fighting during the Munich *Putsch* of 1923 and that Lenin had died of typhus during the First World War. What would the 20th century be like now?

For better or for worse, individuals do make a difference. "The notion that a people can run itself and its affairs anonymously," wrote the philosopher William James, "is now well known to be the silliest of absurdities. Mankind does nothing save through initiatives on the part of inventors, great or small, and imitation by the rest of us—these are the sole factors in human progress. Individuals of genius show the way, and set the patterns, which common people then adopt and follow."

Leadership, James suggests, means leadership in thought as well as in action. In the long run, leaders in thought may well make the greater difference to the world. But, as Woodrow Wilson once said, "Those only are leaders of men, in the general eye, who lead in action. . . . It is at their hands that new thought gets its translation into the crude language of deeds." Leaders in thought often invent in solitude and obscurity, leaving to later generations the tasks of imitation. Leaders in action—the leaders portrayed in this series—have to be effective in their own time.

And they cannot be effective by themselves. They must act in response to the rhythms of their age. Their genius must be adapted, in a phrase of William James's, "to the receptivities of the moment." Leaders are useless without followers. "There goes the mob," said the French politician hearing a clamor in the streets. "I am their leader. I must follow them." Great leaders turn the inchoate emotions of the mob to purposes of their own. They seize on the opportunities of their time, the hopes, fears, frustrations, crises, potentialities.

They succeed when events have prepared the way for them, when the community is waiting to be aroused, when they can provide the clarifying and organizing ideas. Leadership ignites the circuit between the individual and the mass and thereby alters history.

It may alter history for better or for worse. Leaders have been responsible for the most extravagant follies and most monstrous crimes that have beset suffering humanity. They have also been vital in such gains as humanity has made in individual freedom, religious and racial tolerance, social justice and respect for human rights.

There is no sure way to tell in advance who is going to lead for good and who for evil. But a glance at the gallery of men and women in *World Leaders—Past and Present* suggests some useful tests.

One test is this: do leaders lead by force or by persuasion? By command or by consent? Through most of history leadership was exercised by the divine right of authority. The duty of followers was to defer and to obey. "Theirs not to reason why,/ Theirs but to do and die." On occasion, as with the so-called "enlightened despots" of the 18th century in Europe, absolutist leadership was animated by humane purposes. More often, absolutism nourished the passion for domination, land, gold and conquest and resulted in tyranny.

The great revolution of modern times has been the revolution of equality. The idea that all people should be equal in their legal condition has undermined the old structures of authority, hierarchy and deference. The revolution of equality has had two contrary effects on the nature of leadership. For equality, as Alexis de Tocqueville pointed out in his great study *Democracy in America*, might mean equality in servitude as well as equality in freedom.

"I know of only two methods of establishing equality in the political world," Tocqueville wrote. "Rights must be given to every citizen, or none at all to anyone . . . save one, who is the master of all." There was no middle ground "between the sovereignty of all and the absolute power of one man." In his astonishing prediction of 20th-century totalitarian dictatorship, Tocqueville explained how the revolution of equality could lead to the "*Führerprinzip*" and more terrible absolutism than the world had ever known.

But when rights are given to every citizen and the sovereignty of all is established, the problem of leadership takes a new form, becomes more exacting than ever before. It is easy to issue commands and enforce them by the rope and the stake, the concentration camp and the *gulag*. It is much harder to use argument and achievement to overcome opposition and win consent. The Founding Fathers of the United States understood the difficulty. They believed that history had given them the opportunity to decide, as

Alexander Hamilton wrote in the first Federalist Paper, whether men are indeed capable of basing government on "reflection and choice, or whether they are forever destined to depend . . . on accident and force."

Government by reflection and choice called for a new style of leadership and a new quality of followership. It required leaders to be responsive to popular concerns, and it required followers to be active and informed participants in the process. Democracy does not eliminate emotion from politics; sometimes it fosters demagoguery; but it is confident that, as the greatest of democratic leaders put it, you cannot fool all of the people all of the time. It measures leadership by results and retires those who overreach or falter or fail.

It is true that in the long run despots are measured by results too. But they can postpone the day of judgment, sometimes indefinitely, and in the meantime they can do infinite harm. It is also true that democracy is no guarantee of virtue and intelligence in government, for the voice of the people is not necessarily the voice of God. But democracy, by assuring the rights of opposition, offers built-in resistance to the evils inherent in absolutism. As the theologian Reinhold Niebuhr summed it up, "Man's capacity for justice makes democracy possible, but man's inclination to injustice makes democracy necessary."

A second test for leadership is the end for which power is sought. When leaders have as their goal the supremacy of a master race or the promotion of totalitarian revolution or the acquisition and exploitation of colonies or the protection of greed and privilege or the preservation of personal power, it is likely that their leadership will do little to advance the cause of humanity. When their goal is the abolition of slavery, the liberation of women, the enlargement of opportunity for the poor and powerless, the extension of equal rights to racial minorities, the defense of the freedoms of expression and opposition, it is likely that their leadership will increase the sum of human liberty and welfare.

Leaders have done great harm to the world. They have also conferred great benefits. You will find both sorts in this series. Even "good" leaders must be regarded with a certain wariness. Leaders are not demigods; they put on their trousers one leg after another just like ordinary mortals. No leader is infallible, and every leader needs to be reminded of this at regular intervals. Irreverence irritates leaders but is their salvation. Unquestioning submission corrupts leaders and demeans followers. Making a cult of a leader is always a mistake. Fortunately hero worship generates its own antidote. "Every hero," said Emerson, "becomes a bore at last."

The signal benefit the great leaders confer is to embolden the rest of us to live according to our own best selves, to be active, insistent, and resolute in affirming our own sense of things. For great leaders attest to the reality of human freedom against the supposed inevitabilities of history. And they attest to the wisdom and power that may lie within the most unlikely of us, which is why Abraham Lincoln remains the supreme example of great leadership. A great leader, said Emerson, exhibits new possibilities to all humanity. "We feed on genius. . . . Great men exist that there may be greater men."

Great leaders, in short, justify themselves by emancipating and empowering their followers. So humanity struggles to master its destiny, remembering with Alexis de Tocqueville: "It is true that around every man a fatal circle is traced beyond which he cannot pass; but within the wide verge of that circle he is powerful and free; as it is with man, so with communities."

—*New York*

1

Just a Farm Boy

On an early autumn night in 1902 Lev David-ovich Bronstein, a political prisoner of Russia's totalitarian *tsarist* (imperial) regime, planned his escape. In a primitive hut in Verkholensk—one of the dozens of tiny villages above the Arctic Circle in the vast frozen wasteland of the eastern Russian province of Siberia—Lev and his wife and fellow dis-sident, Alexandra, sat discussing his proposed flight to freedom. If successful in his escape at-tempt, Lev would be leaving Siberia but Alexandra would be left behind with their two babies—Zinaida, not yet two years old, and Nina, who was only four months old.

Leaving Alexandra to serve out the last two years of her sentence alone seemed a terrible thing to do. She and Lev had agonized over it for a long time, and finally Alexandra had said, "You can do the movement no good locked away here. Go. I will follow when I can."

Just as it did to Lev, the overthrow of Nicholas II, the hated tsar of Russia, meant more to Alexandra than any personal hardship. Lev's writing, speak-ing, and organizational abilities were needed by the burgeoning revolutionary movement. Both Lev and Alexandra had avidly read *What Is to Be Done?*, a pamphlet by a leading Russian revolutionary named Vladimir Lenin, who was at that time in exile in

Leon Trotsky (1879–1940) was 25 years old when this photograph was made by the tsar's secret police. It be-came part of a government file on people classified as "dangerous anarchists."

A stretch of the Trans-Sibe-rian Railroad, 5,973 miles of track connecting St. Peters-burg (now Leningrad) and the Russian Pacific seaport of Vladivostok. The railway, which crossed the entire width of remote Siberia, was the route to exile for Lev Bronstein—later known as Leon Trotsky—and thou-sands of others convicted as revolutionaries.

The pogrom—an organized massacre of Jews—was a tragically frequent occurrence in Russia's Jewish ghettos. Jews seldom knew when a mob would attack, robbing, beating, even murdering them while, more often than not, the tsarist police simply stood by and permitted the mayhem to continue.

Switzerland. (A copy of this important and influential tract had recently been smuggled in with the village's food shipment.) Lenin argued that the overthrow of the tsar could be accomplished only if a group of disciplined and determined left-wing activists dedicated their lives to the revolution. While in Siberia, Lev had written and secretly distributed many articles and pamphlets that helped the Social Democratic Siberian Union, an organization of railway workers, spread the word about their clandestine group, but these efforts seemed like a drop in the bucket compared to the task of total revolution. If, thought Lev, he could only reach western Europe and join Lenin and the other exiled leaders, he could perhaps play a major part in helping overthrow the tsarist regime. In recent months, several others had managed to flee Verkholensk.

The Siberian villages had been hastily built during a gold rush several years before, and now the rotting huts were used to house political prisoners—those who had dared to oppose the tsar. Although there were no cells or bars, the government needed only a few policemen to patrol the area and prevent escapes. During the long, fierce winters, when temperatures regularly dropped to 55 degrees below zero, nature herself became the ultimate prison guard. To go outside for more than a few minutes meant freezing to death, and freedom was hundreds of miles away across vast, gloomy forests and freezing rivers. Escape was possible only during the brief warmer seasons.

His objections swept aside, he and Alexandra reviewed his escape plan once again. There was perhaps a one in ten chance of succeeding, and, if he was caught, it would mean a life sentence at hard labor. On the night of his escape, shortly after the police inspector had made his usual rounds, a wagon pulled up in back of the hut. The driver was a peasant member of the ever-increasing Russian underground movement. There was a last hasty farewell, a last caress of each sleeping baby. Lev concealed himself beneath the load of hay and the wagon rattled off into the night.

Police raid the St. Petersburg office of a Nihilist publication in the 1890s. Nihilism, one of the more violent of the many revolutionary movements that sprang up in late 19th-century Russia, aimed at achieving political change through terrorism.

A Nihilist bomb takes the life of Tsar Alexander II (1818–1881) in St. Petersburg. Alexander had freed Russia's serfs (peasants who were practically slaves of wealthy landowners), reformed the nation's legal system, and founded many schools. Despite these liberal reforms, his reign was marked by growing revolutionary and terroristic movements, and numerous attempts were made to assassinate him.

He arrived penniless at the first stop, hundreds of miles away in Irkutsk, the village where in 1900 he and Alexandra had begun their exile. All of their money had been left with Alexandra so that she could feed the children until the next government check arrived. In Irkutsk, friends gave him pocket money, a suitcase containing some clothing, and a priceless forged passport with a blank line for a new name.

For his name he chose Leon Trotsky. Trotsky was a Russian derivation of the German name Trotz, and it meant boldness, defiance, confidence, insolence, disdain—all terms later applied as both insults and compliments to the revolutionary leader.

Lev soon boarded the Trans-Siberian railway for the second stage of his long, difficult journey. He knew that at any moment he could be pulled roughly from his seat and sent back to Siberia. He did not know that he would one day change history. He was to become one of the leaders of a revolution that would seek to replace worldwide capitalism (the economic system based on private enterprise) with socialism (the economic system based on government ownership of the means of production). Nor did he know that he was to earn a reputation as a military genius, forging a band of tattered peasants and workers into a powerful army and leading it to victory—or that he would die violently, a man without a country, forever hated in his beloved Russia.

At first glance there would seem to be little in Lev Bronstein's background that would transform him into Leon Trotsky. His isolated and somewhat privileged childhood could just as easily have molded him into becoming a successful farmer or engineer. He was born on October 26, 1879, in a tiny village called Yanovka, on the southern steppes—vast, treeless prairies—of the Ukraine, the wheat belt of Russia. His parents were Jews, and that fact in itself could have made a significant difference. Since the 16th century, when Tsar Ivan the Terrible had offered the country's Jewish population a choice between conversion to Christianity or death by drowning, Russian Jews had been denied all human rights and had thus been forced to live precariously, perched between survival and the threat of annihilation.

By the end of the 19th century, almost all of Russia's Jewish population had been herded into an area between the Black and Baltic seas called the "Pale of Settlement." (A pale is an officially designated restricted area, generally established for the purpose of confining, and limiting the movements of, ethnic minorities.) They were not allowed to travel or change their residence. Some became craftsmen, some traders; and a few managed to hire themselves out as wage laborers.

Many of the more educated young men and women from the Pale became active in struggles to bring democracy to Russia. Some joined an organization called *Zemlya i Volya*—Land and Freedom—and lived among the peasants while trying to persuade them to revolt against the tsar. This particular revolutionary experiment proved disastrous, however, since the vast majority of the *muzhiks* (peasants) were extremely conservative, idolized the tsar, and did not like being told that they were in need of "enlightenment." By the year of Lev Bronstein's birth, those young activists who had not

Anna Bronstein (d. 1910). Overworked and often exhausted, Anna displayed little outward warmth toward Trotsky when he was young. In later years, however, she was able to make clear the deep love she felt for both her son and his children.

Although Trotsky and his father, David Leontievich Bronstein (1850–1922), often disagreed violently, there were strong bonds of affection and respect between the two. In his autobiography, Trotsky praised his father's "unusually good eye both for things and people."

been betrayed to the tsarist police by the very peasants they had hoped to help were beginning to leave the organization and turn instead to terrorist activity, dynamiting public buildings in an effort to wake up the populace.

The Ukraine was the one area where some Jews had been permitted to settle and work the land. Lev's father, David Leontievich Bronstein, had moved there with his family during one of the lulls in the ongoing persecution of Russian Jews. Through hard work and extreme thrift he had managed to accumulate some money. Just before Lev's birth, he and his wife Anna had bought 250 acres and leased another 400 from the local landlord, a retired Russian army colonel named Yanovsky.

Lev and his family lived in a mud hut that had five small rooms and a roof thatched with straw. The parents labored alongside their workers from dawn to dusk and staggered home exhausted at the end of each day. Every extra penny was used to obtain still more land and farm animals. David Bronstein became, through his own efforts, Yanovka's chief employer and only flour-mill owner.

The thatched hut was by no means a luxurious or even comfortable place to live. When it rained, the children scurried to get pots and pans to collect the water that leaked from the straw roof onto the dirt floor. Snakes and fleas infested the rickety walls and the dilapidated roof. Tall visitors had to be careful not to crack their heads on the low rafters. It was not until Lev was 17 and no longer lived at home that his parents were able to build a pleasant and substantial brick house.

More than he felt deprived of material benefits, however, Lev felt emotionally deprived. His industrious parents had little time to spend with their children.

Despite what he called the atmosphere of his "grayish" childhood, Lev enjoyed playing with his brother and sisters and, later, helping his parents by keeping their accounts at the mill. The summers were particularly beautiful, with roses and flowering acacias almost covering the small hut. Living in the country taught Lev an appreciation of solitude, and

> *The land, the cattle, the poultry, the mill, took all my parents' time; there was none left for us. The seasons succeeded one another, and waves of farm work swept over domestic affection.*
> —LEON TROTSKY
> in *My Life*, his autobiography, describing his childhood in the Ukraine

the lack of affection only developed in him a more affectionate attitude toward others. From his father, he learned such values as hard work, thrift, neatness, and a strict sense of careful organization. From his mother, Anna Bronstein, he undoubtedly gained his love of books.

Anna had grown up in an urban area. She had fallen in love with the handsome and graceful David Bronstein and married him despite her parents' disapproval of the illiterate young farmer. By the time Lev was born, Anna was constantly fatigued and aging prematurely. She had given birth to eight children. Diphtheria and scarlet fever had killed four of them in infancy. Lev grew up with a brother, Alexander, and two sisters, Elizabetta and Olga. Lev's sisters taught him how to read and do sums before he ever went to school. On long winter evenings, Anna Bronstein would read aloud from novels she took from the library.

It would seem on the surface that being Jewish had no effect on Lev, but if he had not been a Jew, he might have lived out his life peacefully on the Bronstein farm. As it was, since Russia's anti-Semitic laws prohibited his going to a state school, he had to leave the farm in order to get an education.

The great famine of 1891 resulted in bread lines for a lucky few and death by starvation for tens of thousands of other Russian peasants. Although the tsarist government made no effort to relieve their sufferings, the nation's peasants were unreceptive to revolutionary ideas.

At the age of seven Lev was sent to a Jewish day school in the nearby town of Gromokla, where he stayed with his Aunt Rachel and Uncle Abram. His parents paid for his keep with farm products. Lev made no friends. The children spoke Yiddish, a German-derived language spoken by many Russian and eastern European Jews, while Lev spoke a mixture of Russian and Ukrainian. Homesick and unhappy, Lev developed frequent stomach trouble, a problem that would plague him for the rest of his life. Nevertheless, he eagerly soaked up everything the school had to offer.

It was also in Gromokla that Lev had his first substantial confrontation with social inequality. Divided by a ravine, the town had two distinct sides. Later Lev remembered that the houses in the German section "were neat, partly roofed with tile and partly with reeds, the horses large, the cows sleek." In contrast, on the Jewish side of the ravine, "the cabins were dilapidated, the roofs tattered, the cattle scrawny."

Lev's next important political lesson came when his mother's nephew, Moissei Filipovich Spentzer (called Monya by the family) came from Odessa to spend a summer on the farm recovering from an illness. A liberal, open-minded intellectual who had worked as a journalist and statistician, Monya immediately took a liking to Lev and spent the summer attempting to improve his clever country cousin's level of sophistication. He gave Lev lessons in table manners, tutored him in grammar to improve his rural, rather uncouth Russian, and taught him arithmetic that went beyond the simple addition required for keeping accounts on the farm. More important, at the dinner table Lev listened raptly as Monya talked about Odessa's cultural life, and about books, injustices under tsarism, and the need for democracy and freedom.

With education for Lev a dead end in the Yanovka area, his parents eagerly accepted an offer made by Monya the following year. Monya had married an educated woman, Fanny, the principal of the State School for Jewish Girls, and Lev was invited to live in the city of Odessa with them and their new baby

Leo Tolstoy (1828–1910) was one of the many authors whose works were eagerly absorbed by the young Trotsky. Best known for his great novels *War and Peace* and *Anna Karenina*, Tolstoy was also a Christian philosopher and an advocate of social reform in Russia.

daughter while he went to school. It was hard to go so far away from home, and Lev cried when he parted with his family, but his homesickness quickly disappeared. The busy and sophisticated Black Sea port of Odessa was very exciting to the nine-year-old boy, so used to the quiet of the countryside.

The Spentzers' apartment was small, and Lev's bed was behind a curtain in a corner of the dining room. He was strictly disciplined. His aunt and uncle placed great emphasis on cleanliness, good table manners, and proper speech. The rules may have seemed excessive to Lev, but there were many compensations. For the first time, he was surrounded by love and affection. He played for hours with the Spentzers' baby daughter, who was just three weeks old when Lev arrived, cooing and singing to her as he rocked her cradle. Later he helped her through her first steps and then taught her how to read. His natural intelligence developed in the atmosphere of the Spentzers' household. Late into the night he read the works of such famous authors as Tolstoy, Goethe, Dickens, and Pushkin, and discussed the books with Monya and Fanny.

Despite his high grades and abilities, even Fanny Spentzer's influence could not win him, a Jewish boy, admission to the *Gymnasium*, or classical school. He went instead to the less fashionable *Real-schule*, which emphasized mathematics and science. At the head of his class, he tutored other boys in order to earn money to attend the opera.

His love of writing surfaced early as well. Late into the night he scrawled commentaries on the day's events. Soon he was proudly sporting spectacles, believing that they made him look older and more intellectual.

By the time Lev was 10, there was already a glimmer of rebellion in his eyes, reflecting his embryonic awareness of the need to take a stand against injustice. When a teacher named Burnaude treated a slower student in a cruel way, Lev organized a protest, in which students drove their teacher into a rage by making a howling noise with their mouths closed. The next day, the teacher found some stu-

Life under conditions in Siberia was not easy, and my escape would place a double burden on the shoulders of Alexandra Lvovna. But she met this objection with two words: 'You must.' Duty to the revolution overshadowed everything else for her, personal relations especially.
—LEON TROTSKY
recalling his wife's acceptance of his escape from exile in Siberia in 1902

dents willing to declare that Lev had been the instigator of this escapade.

The Spentzers came to school to plead Lev's case, but the principal was in no mood for leniency. "He has all the boys in the school in his power. That boy is going to be a dangerous member of society. He is a moral monster!" he told them, and expelled Lev for the rest of the term.

Terrified of displeasing his father, Lev persuaded the Spentzers to keep the news from his family, but finally his parents had to be told that he would be returning home for the rest of the term. When he arrived at the farm, his father at first refused to speak to him. But soon David Bronstein approached Lev and said sternly, "Show me how you whistled at your headmaster." Clearly proud of his son's boldness, he roared with laughter when Lev demonstrated.

Lev returned to Odessa the next term, but things were not the same. The cowed and excessively obedient behavior of the other boys, including some of those who had previously been his friends, shocked him deeply. He always remembered it as an important lesson in understanding human character and behavior.

In 1894, by which time Lev had been living with Monya and Fanny for six years, some important events made him more conscious of the world around him. That year Tsar Alexander III died. A group of liberal intellectuals, of which Monya and Fanny were members, appealed to the new tsar, Nicholas II, for a constitution and some guarantees of democracy. The tsar responded by dismissing their request as "nonsensical dreams."

But the Spentzers were not to remain his single greatest influence. As events unfolded, he was gradually to abandon all faith in the usefulness of constitutional reforms. Increasingly, Lev came to consider outright revolution the only effective way of achieving radical political change.

In 1896 Lev reached his sixth and last term at his school, St. Paul's. The only way he could finish high school was to leave the Spentzers and move to Nikolayev, a city 75 miles northeast of Odessa, on a river that emptied into the Black Sea. If another school in Odessa had accepted him, there might never have been a Leon Trotsky. For it was in Nikolayev that he fell in love, became a revolutionary, and wound up in the prisons of the tsar and the wastes of Siberia with a wife and two children, all before his 22nd birthday. Later, Leon Trotsky would call that year the turning point of his youth: "It raised within me the question of my place in human society."

Tsar Alexander III (1845–1894), and his six children, one of whom (rear center) would succeed him as Nicholas II (1868–1918), the last of the Romanov dynasty. Rigidly religious and extremely conservative, Alexander encouraged persecution of the Jews and canceled many of the liberal reforms instituted by his father, Alexander II.

2

Love and Prison Bars

Arriving in Nikolayev, the 17-year-old Lev took up lodgings with strangers. Without the loving friendship of the Spentzers, a strong and lasting depression seized him for the first time in his life. Nothing seemed to appeal to him; he had no commitment to anything, no idea of what to do with himself after graduation. He avidly read everything he could get his hands on—history, philosophy, literature—everything except his assigned lessons.

Perhaps if he had arrived in Nikolayev during a quieter period, he would have gone on to become an engineer or teacher. However, these were not peaceful times. All over the town, many small groups were secretly meeting to discuss the situations then arising both in Russia and beyond the nation's borders. Such intense intellectual activity was inevitable in a town like Nikolayev, which had a large population of educated Germans and Jews.

Because Nikolayev was a port, peasants came there to sell their produce, and their worsening situation had begun to become painfully obvious. The development of new agricultural technology in more industrially advanced countries like the United States had driven down the price of grain on the

Karl Marx (1818–1883), the German political philosopher whose writings formed the basis of the communist movement. As a student in Nikolayev, Trotsky studied Marx's works, including his masterpiece, *Das Kapital*. However, the young revolutionary did not believe Marx's program would bring about change quickly enough.

By the time he was 17, the future Leon Trotsky had adopted both pince-nez eyeglasses, which were to become his trademark, and the belief—to which he remained committed for the rest of his life—that revolution was the only route to a better life for the working classes of the world.

Russian revolutionary Vladimir Lenin (seated at center; 1870–1924) and Yulii Martov (right; 1873–1923), cofounders of the League of Struggle for the Liberation of the Working Class, with fellow members in 1895. Soon after this photograph was taken, the young revolutionaries—who were to form the nucleus of the Communist party—were deported to Siberia.

world markets. Always poor, the Russian grain growers were now at the brink of starvation.

In 1896 the news seeped in that a workers' strike in St. Petersburg, the Russian capital, had been brutally put down by the tsar's dreaded cossack regiments, cavalry formations that were the ruling regime's first line of defense against insurrection. As a result, many St. Petersburg students had become even more deeply involved in protest movements against the repressive Russian government.

In the home where Lev rented a room, the landlady's sons enthusiastically discussed politics over every meal. Then, for the first time, Lev was introduced to the many varieties of socialist ideas in Rus-

sia. He came to agree that such socialist proposals as the common ownership of the factories and the land by workers and peasants were laudable, but he did not believe that the tsar would ever willingly relinquish his power. Lev's convictions thus ran counter to those of the landlady's sons, who were members of a political group known as the Populists, who believed that progressive Russians could create a better society without recourse to violent revolution.

At about this time Lev had also come to learn of the existence of socialists who called themselves Marxists. This group was named after Karl Marx, the 19th-century German philosopher and social and economic theorist who had declared, among other things, that the workers of Russia would have to be educated politically if they were to stand a chance of overthrowing the government and setting up a socialist system. Lev's knowledge of Marxism was at that time limited to its insistence that all aspects of a society are determined by its economic condition. To the young and highly individualistic rebel from Yanovka, Marxism seemed to view men and women as impotent prisoners of their social and economic situation, only to be freed by a long, slow process of education. It is not surprising that someone with Lev's boundless energy and imagination found the Marxist approach stuffy and dry. Then there were the Social-Revolutionaries, who believed that revolution could be achieved only through terrorist actions, such as kidnapping and assassination. Lev believed that their approach was basically self-destructive.

Thinking, reading, and arguing about changing the world interested and excited Lev more than any of his formal studies. A school friend, impressed with Lev's debating skills, one day brought him to an isolated orchard, rented by a Czech gardener named Franz Shvigovsky. Franz had organized a student circle that met regularly in the orchard.

Franz was 28, with a full beard and rich voice, and Lev was immediately impressed with his deep commitment to social change. Although he clearly had the talent to have pursued a successful career, he chose to remain poor. Gardening gave him time to do what he loved best—read, study, learn, and discuss ways to change the world. In addition, Franz could read German, and had a thorough knowledge of the classics. His library was crammed with political books and foreign newspapers outlawed by the tsar.

The members of the discussion circle called themselves "the nursery gardeners." They wore blue workmen's uniforms and round straw hats and carried crudely carved black walking sticks. Lev's interest in radical politics grew as he sat in on the weekly meetings with his new friends in the orchard. There they heatedly debated world events, ate apples and fresh vegetables from Shvigovsky's garden, and drank endless pots of tea.

There was one Marxist in the circle—Alexandra Lvovna Sokolovskaya. Six years Lev's senior, the 23-year-old Alexandra had far more experience in politics and life. She had been raised by a poverty-stricken father who was a supporter of the Social-Revolutionaries and a firm believer in liberty. At the University of Odessa, she had taken a course in midwifery and had met Marxist students who had worked with exiled Russian Marxists in Geneva, Switzerland. Her brothers, Grigory and Ilya, also members of the group, had told Alexandra that Lev was a brilliant debater—logical and unbeatable.

Lev had never met a young woman with intelligence and wit that matched his own, and Alexandra could not help being impressed by Lev's sharp mind and articulate speech. As the two of them debated fiercely in the orchard, they began to fall in love.

Despite their differences concerning methods, "the nursery gardeners" all agreed that the overthrow of the tsar and the establishment of socialism was their primary goal. Deciding that mere talk was almost completely useless, they attempted to act publicly. Renaming themselves the Universal Knowledge Association, with their senior member, Franz, as the director and Lev as the secretary, they hired a hall, which they filled with an interested, non-paying audience. Lev delivered his first speech, a disorganized, rambling monologue that was to-

The farther east one goes in Europe, the more the bourgeoisie becomes in the political respect weaker, more cowardly, and meaner, and the larger are the cultural and political tasks which fall as the share of the proletariat.
—quoted from the founding manifesto of the Russian Social-Democratic Labor party, March 1898

tally incomprehensible to his listeners.

Later that same year, 1896, David Bronstein came to Nikolayev to market his wheat and check up on his son's progress. When Lev excitedly told his father about the illegal group he had joined, and described the wonderful people he had met, David Bronstein was frightened. It was one thing for a young boy to show disrespect for a harsh teacher,

Alexandra Lvovna Sokolovskaya (1873—c.1938) rests an arm on the shoulder of her future husband, Lev Bronstein (Trotsky), after a meeting of the "nursery gardeners," the revolutionary discussion group to which they belonged, in Nikolayev in 1897. At left is Alexandra's brother Ilya.

but quite another for a teenaged student to take on the tsarist regime.

A terrible argument ensued, with the father shouting and shaking his fists and the son stubbornly refusing to stop his activities or desert his friends. Threatened with the loss of his father's financial support unless he gave in, Lev walked away from his father without so much as saying farewell. With Alexandra's brothers and three other students, he rented a tiny cabin from Franz. By sharing food and working as a tutor, Lev managed to survive.

Despite the fact that he devoted much of his time to political activities, Lev graduated with honors in the summer of 1897. He then traveled home to Yanovka to make peace with his father. Once again, however, they had a bitter quarrel. David Bronstein wanted his son to attend the University of Odessa to study engineering. But by now Lev had only one burning interest, to turn the corrupt tsarist state into the first socialist country in the world.

A short time later, a wealthy uncle from Odessa made Lev an offer that was impossible to refuse. His uncle's house was open to him. He could take a few courses at the university while making up his mind about his future. Money would be no problem; the uncle owned a boiler factory. Lev traveled back to Odessa but the new arrangement did not last long. He argued constantly with his uncle about conditions in the boiler factory. At first his uncle said Lev would outgrow his ideas—that in 10 years he would forget his radical notions. But when Lev actually attempted to play the part of an agitator and persuade the boiler factory's workers to take industrial action, his uncle became infuriated and told him to leave. Lev returned to the Spentzers. Not wanting to impose upon them financially, he took a job in a tutoring school, all the while hungering for his "gardeners" in Nikolayev, especially Alexandra. Perhaps hoping to be fired, he began to attend work wearing unconventional clothes and long hair. He was soon dismissed, but decided to remain in Odessa.

After several other student radicals had been arrested and banished to Siberia, Lev finally decided to return to his friends in Nikolayev. He and Alexandra's brother, Grigory, agreed that the workers were the only people with the power to overthrow the tsar, and that students and other intellectuals should stop their theorizing and instead start to organize the region's workers into a union.

About 10,000 workers were employed at the docks and in the two big factories in Nikolayev. Lev met potential recruits to the union-organizing group in a tavern where the organ played so loudly that their conversations about socialism could not be overheard by police spies.

At night the handful of revolutionaries worked on their one-page newspaper, *Our Cause*. They had no typewriters, so they hand-printed their articles on stencils and ran off copies on a primitive mimeograph machine. Matches and a can of kerosene were

At the beginning of the 20th century, most of Russia's peasants—the bulk of its population—were still using medieval agricultural tools and techniques. Illiterate, superstitious, and at the mercy of the landowner in whose fields he labored, the peasant had little to look forward to but ever-deepening poverty.

Alexander Herzen (1812–1870), writer (*My Past and Thoughts*, *Who is to Blame?*), intellectual, and philosopher, was also publisher of *The Bell*, a revolutionary newspaper. His brilliant and scathing denunciations of the tsarist system strongly influenced generations of liberals and socialists, including the young Leon Trotsky.

always kept close at hand so that the leaflets and the printing machine could quickly be burned should the police raid the office.

Lev and the others took turns taking the night ferry to Odessa, where they would hand out the tracts and gather information. Workmen would tell the young revolutionaries their grievances over wages and work conditions, and 24 hours later they would see their complaints set out in *Our Cause*. Lev was a whirlwind of energy and enthusiasm. He could go nights and days without sleep, writing, working at the printing machine, attending meetings. Members of the group would stay up until dawn, discussing how best they might counter government spies, trying to resolve disputes over the content of their next broadsheet, and arguing about the most efficient way to expand their range of contacts and associates.

As a result of this increased activity by Lev and his comrades, the police began to pay more attention to them. The revolutionaries had recruited over 200 members, who met in separate groups of 25, with a lookout and a signal system to warn them if the police were about to pounce. That way, it was reasoned, if one group was arrested, the others could carry on the work. The factory owners, furious at the appearance of the group's effective, purple-inked, mimeographed newsletters, reacted with propaganda leaflets of their own, and urged the police to move in.

It was amazing that the union functioned as long as it did. The police found it impossible to believe that the agitation in Nikolayev was the work of a group of "kids." They planted spies in the organization and told the infiltrators to discover the real brains behind the unionization campaign. The spies finally confirmed that it was indeed the beardless 19-year-old and a handful of others who led the group. The police decided to round them up.

Shvigovsky had left the garden and was working on an estate outside the city. Lev, on his way back from a visit to his family, stopped to see him on January 27, 1898. They were talking in the house when the police stormed in and arrested them.

The next day there were mass raids. Two hundred people were seized and taken away in chains. Alexandra was out of town, but when she heard the news, she returned and gave herself up to the police.

The Nikolayev prison was the first of many jails that Lev was to inhabit. There, as later, he snatched at every opportunity to read, teach, think, and plan for the future revolution. To keep warm in the ice-cold cell, Lev paced up and down, discussing and arguing with his cellmate, a radical bookbinder. He was not brought to trial and had received no word from his friends. The police had separated them, hoping to break their spirit, holding their treatment up as a warning to other young people who might be tempted to challenge the authorities. They were not allowed to consult with lawyers, to have books, to receive or to send mail, or to have visitors. Yet Lev did not seem to regret his chosen path. In three weeks he was transferred to a jail in Kherson, a small town 75 miles southeast of Nikolayev; the worst was yet to come.

Placed in solitary confinement in a dark, cold cell, Lev had no pencils, paper, or books. Lice infested every hair on his body. The food was terrible—a little stale bread, some salt, and a meager, tasteless helping of stew.

It took Lev's mother three months to find out where he was. She had to bribe the guards before they would agree to see that Lev received the gifts she had brought; ordinary things that seemed incredibly precious to a man in the condition to which her son had been reduced—a pillow, a blanket, bread, tea, sugar, jam, fruit, soap, a comb.

In March 1898, while Lev still languished in prison at Kherson, nine radicals had met in the city of Minsk and established the All-Russian Social-Democratic Labor party. They published a program (one that Lev would later accept) which called for a two-stage revolution in Russia. First, the country would be made a democracy and its industrial base greatly developed and expanded by the *bourgeoisie*—the social class that Marx's colleague Friedrich Engels had defined as "the class of modern capitalists, owners of the means of social production

The working class? I know of no such class in Russia. Sergei Yulevich, I do not understand what you are talking about. We have peasants. They form ninety percent of the population. . . . You are trying to create artificially a new class, a sort of social relationship completely alien to Russia. In this respect, you are a dangerous socialist.
—K. P. POBEDONOSTSEV leading Russian churchman, to Count Sergei Yulevich Witte, finance minister

and employers of wage labor." Next would come the socialist revolution, led by the workers.

In May 1898 Lev was transferred to the prison at Odessa, where the warder was a huge man called Trotsky. One of the Sokolovsky brothers was in the next cell, and they were able to communicate by tapping on water pipes or by shouting through the windows. Allowed books from the prison library, Lev read the works of the 18th-century French liberal polemicist Voltaire, the 18th-century German philosopher Immanuel Kant, and Charles Darwin, the 19th-century British naturalist who first formulated the theory of evolution by natural selection.

Discovering that Alexandra was also housed in the huge jail, Lev wrote her a romantic note proposing marriage, but his father quickly put a stop to that by sending off a telegram to the Ministry of Justice in St. Petersburg, refusing to give his underage son permission to marry.

In the fall of 1899, Lev, Alexandra, her brothers, and the other union organizers were transferred to a Moscow prison. At last, in early 1900, after two years without a trial, they were brought in to face their judges. In those days trials of political prisoners were a sham. Dossiers would be compiled by the police and then the Ministry of Justice in St. Petersburg would hand down the orders to be followed—release, imprisonment, or exile. All the leading "nursery gardeners" were sentenced to four years of exile in eastern Siberia.

Even then, their sentences did not begin right away. They were kept six more months in the Moscow transfer prison. Now they were allowed to walk together for half an hour each day and to visit the bath house. In the spring, Alexandra and Lev were married by a Jewish chaplain in a cell, using a ring borrowed from a guard. This time, David Bronstein, knowing that the young people would not be able to live together after they were transferred to Siberia unless they were legally married, did not interfere. Meanwhile, still separated, they slept on boards in the prison.

At the transfer prison the young revolutionaries continued their debates and studies, spending

much time reading the works of Vladimir Ilich Ulyanov, a young radical intellectual who was at that
time gaining prominence in Marxist circles and had
been imprisoned in 1895 for his membership in a
St. Petersburg organization which called itself the
League of Struggle for the Liberation of the Working
Class. For relaxation, Lev and his fellow detainees
played a Russian version of tennis in the prison
yard. Even in confinement, Lev showed his qualities
of courage, good cheer, and leadership. He planned
and carried out a hunger strike and other demonstrations for prisoners' rights. His fellow prisoners
began to view him as a man without fear, yet gentle
and kind, who often kissed and embraced his
friends.

Preparing to embark on his long and bitter journey to Siberia, a political prisoner mutely submits to the placing of heavy chains around his wrists and ankles. The "crimes" committed by many exiles were often no worse than reading officially forbidden books or taking part in political discussion groups.

It was not until the fall of 1900, when they began the long trip to Siberia, that Lev and Alexandra were able to be together. They traveled northward along the Mongolian border and then were transferred to a convict barge on the Lena River.

All along the waterway, exiles were dropped off one or two at a time in tiny villages. Lev and Alexandra were put off at a settlement of about 100 huts called Ust-Kut. Here, cockroaches and rats far outnumbered people. The inhabitants' only recreation was heavy drinking. In the winter, the temperature dropped to 55 degrees below zero, and in the spring and fall the village turned into a sea of mud.

Lev, never athletic, learned to fish and hunt. He also sold a few articles to a provincial newspaper. When he was offered a job as a clerk for a wealthy fur merchant, Lev was allowed to take his wife and new baby daughter to a somewhat less unpleasant village, 100 miles to the east. When Lev was fired for a bookkeeping error, they went back to Ust-Kut.

The Lena River was like a connecting railway between exiled revolutionaries. Messages were sent from village to village, and in the summer the exiles gathered on the riverbanks to trade rumors. As the movement against the tsar spread, more and more political prisoners arrived in Siberia, bringing fresh news with them. In 1901 the exiles learned that peasants had rioted in southern Russia. The Social-Revolutionary terrorists had also stepped up their activities. In February the minister of education was assassinated; in April, the minister of the interior.

Lev played an important role in composing a statement, printed by the exiles, that declared terrorism futile. The tsar, said the statement, could always appoint a new minister, or construct a new building to replace one that had been blown up. Only a disciplined group of professional revolutionaries, the statement continued, could have any hope of toppling the tsar's regime, and only masses of people could change society permanently. In western Europe, exiled Russian revolutionaries saw the statement and were deeply impressed by Lev's writing. He became known as "The Pen."

In 1902 Lev and Alexandra received permission

to transfer to Verkholensk, a larger settlement for political prisoners. At night they sat around bonfires on the banks of the Lena, reading aloud. Under a pseudonym, Lev wrote articles for the publication of the Siberian railwaymen. That summer, he learned about *Iskra* (*The Spark*), a new and important Marxist newspaper published in Zurich, Switzerland, by a small group of exiled Russian dissidents headed by Ulyanov, who had by this time taken the revolutionary name Lenin.

The Russian government undoubtedly believed that four years in Siberia would have weakened the resolve of the hotheaded young radicals. Indeed, many were broken by their experience; some even committed suicide. But Lev was a rare man, one committed to history. In an essay entitled "Optimism and Pessimism," composed early in 1901, he wrote: "As long as I breathe, I shall fight for the future, that radiant future in which man, strong and beautiful, will become master of the drifting stream of his history and will direct it towards the boundless horizon of beauty, joy, and happiness. . . ."

It became increasingly imperative for the strongly motivated young idealist to leave behind the limited work in Siberia and begin to play a bigger role in the revolutionary movement. It was then that he and Alexandra decided that he must escape.

Newly released political prisoners prepare to leave Siberia after the 1917 Russian Revolution. Although the new Soviet government quickly gave amnesty to the political dissidents who had been exiled by the tsar, it was soon sending a stream of its own victims to the icy vastness of Siberia.

3

Dress Rehearsal for Revolution

> *Revolution is an expression of the impossibility of reconstructing society by rationalist methods. Logical arguments are impotent against material interests.*
> —LEON TROTSKY

Lev Bronstein, dedicated revolutionary and recent escapee from detention as a political prisoner, disembarked from the Trans-Siberian Railway at Samara, a town on the Volga River where *Iskra* had located its Russian office. The newspaper's supporters formed the nucleus of the Russian Social-Democratic Labor party, which included both Russian political exiles in several western European countries and activists inside Russia. Wherever these revolutionary groups existed, Trotsky found friends to help him—in 1902 and throughout his life. The *Iskra* staff members in Samara had been much impressed by his articles. Night after night he and his new friends sat around the *samovar* (a Russian tea urn) discussing the political situation. When the message came from Lenin asking Lev, who was now known as Leon Trotsky, to join the *Iskra* staff, these new friends, despite their lack of funds, gave him money and arranged for his escape over the Russian border and into Austria.

It was a difficult journey, filled with close calls that could have landed him back in police custody, but his luck held. By the time he boarded the night train

The beautiful and strong-willed Natalya Ivanova Sedova (1882–1962) was 19 when she met Trotsky in Paris. She remained by his side until his death 39 years later, but, demonstrating the true revolutionary's disdain for middle-class "respectability," she never married him. Trotsky's legal wife, Alexandra, even became good friends with Natalya.

A Russian peasant family takes time out for a song on the balalaika, a guitarlike instrument traditional in Russia for centuries. Trotsky's controversial belief—that socialism could be achieved in Russia without undergoing various stages of democratic development—was based in part on the fact that Russian society remained primitive.

for Vienna, all his money had been spent on guides and the train ticket. In Vienna, Victor Adler, the leader of the Austrian Social Democrats, gave Trotsky money to get to Zurich, Lenin's headquarters. When he arrived in Zurich, Trotsky learned that Lenin and other *Iskra* staff members had gone on to London. With just enough money to get to Paris and across the English Channel, Trotsky finally reached London in October 1902. He arrived in a taxi, penniless, at 10 Holford Square, just before dawn.

Inside the building, Lenin and his wife, Nadezhda Konstantinovna Krupskaya, lived as Mr. and Mrs. Jacob Richter in one scantily furnished room. Krupskaya, who was in charge of the secret couriers who had made contact with Trotsky in Siberia, opened the door in her nightclothes and called to Lenin, still in bed: "The Pen has arrived!"

Lenin was 10 years older than Trotsky and from a very different background. His parents were professionals and he had been raised in cities. In 1887 his brother Alexander had been hanged for conspiring to assassinate the tsar. Although Lenin was admitted to the bar four years later, he never practiced law. Instead he organized study circles in St. Petersburg and fell in love with Krupskaya, one of the students in his circle. In 1895 he became ill and went to western Europe to recover. There he

Led by Russian Orthodox priest George Gapon, St. Petersburg workers carry a petition to the tsar on "Bloody Sunday"—January 22, 1905. The ensuing massacre of the peaceful marchers by the tsar's troops enlisted the world's sympathy. American author Mark Twain wrote: "If such a government cannot be overthrown otherwise than by dynamite, then thank God for dynamite."

met many exiled Russian revolutionaries. By the time he returned home, he too was a revolutionary. Following his arrest in 1895, he wrote pamphlets while he was in jail that gained him fame both in Russia and abroad. Krupskaya married him and accompanied him into exile in Siberia. In 1900, his sentence over, they went to Switzerland to publish *Iskra*.

The morning after Trotsky arrived in London, while Lenin took him on a tour of the city, Krupskaya arranged for his lodgings in a rooming house where other revolutionaries were living. Trotsky quickly made friends with Yulii Martov, a witty, talkative man and a cofounder, with Lenin, of the St. Petersburg League of Struggle for the Liberation of the Working Class. In a day or two, he started on his writing assignments. The rest of the *Iskra* staff quickly noted Trotsky's talent, and he was asked to give a public lecture. This time, far more knowledgeable than he had been when he gave his maiden speech to the "nursery gardeners," Trotsky demonstrated a remarkable speaking ability. He was soon sent on a lecture tour of Brussels, Liège, and Paris.

It was in Paris, only months after he had said farewell to Alexandra and his two baby daughters, that Trotsky met a talented and beautiful young woman named Natalya Ivanovna Sedova. Natalya had also been born in the Ukraine. Orphaned when she was eight, she had spent most of her life in boarding schools. She had been expelled from her last school for demonstrating against compulsory religious observance, and had moved to Geneva to study. There she had been recruited by the Social-Democrats and had been sent to Paris as part of the chain of people smuggling Marxist literature into Russia.

Natalya had been inspired by Trotsky's writings and found him even more exciting in person. The attraction was intense and mutual and they soon became lovers. Trotsky never divorced Alexandra, and in later years they remained friends, but for the rest of his life he lived with Natalya, who bore him two sons.

From a bridge, Lenin pointed out Westminster [the Houses of Parliament]. . . . 'This is their famous Westminster,' [he said] and 'their' referred of course not to the English but to the ruling classes. To his eyes, the invisible shadow of the ruling classes always overlay the whole of human culture— a shadow that was as real to him as daylight.
—LEON TROTSKY
recalling the first day of his stay in London in 1902 with fellow revolutionary Vladimir Lenin

During the short time that he had been in western Europe, Trotsky had become increasingly aware of disputes within the revolutionary organization that might come to threaten its efficiency if they went unresolved. Along with the atmosphere of comradeship and cooperation that permeated life in the party, there was also a tendency toward factionalism and rivalry. In the summer of 1903, the All-Russian Social-Democratic Labor party met for its second congress.

A major disagreement about the nature of the party split the congress. Lenin, believing that the task of overthrowing the tsarist government required a highly disciplined organization, wanted the party to be open only to active and committed revolutionaries who were willing to accept the discipline of a central leadership. This meant that all of the loosely knit groups in Russia would come under the command of one leadership. Martov and the others wanted the party to be open to anyone who supported its program. Each small unit would retain its own autonomy, and all would function as equals without any centralized authority.

Trotsky sided with Lenin on the issue of centralized authority, but he allied himself with his friend Martov on the standards for membership. He earned the reputation at that congress for sharpness and sarcasm in his debating style. "Lenin's methods," he told the assembled delegates, "lead to this: the party organization will substitute itself for the party as a whole; then the central committee will take the place of the organization; and finally a single dictator will take the place of the central committee."

Lenin's group, the *Bolsheviks*, or majority, won the vote; but Martov's group, the *Mensheviks*, or minority, boycotted the central committee. The *Iskra* staff kept changing hands, and Trotsky found himself caught in the ideological crossfire. He was against the hesitant and liberal "inconsistency" (as Lenin later put it) that began to infuse Menshevik ranks, but he also opposed the "consistent," rigid centralism of Lenin and the Bolsheviks.

A few months later, historic events intruded. In February 1904 the Japanese navy staged a surprise attack on Russian ships at Port Arthur, thus launching the 1904—05 Russo-Japanese war for colonies in Asia. Thousands of young men were killed, and the tsar's armies were decisively defeated. Russian soldiers, angry and demoralized, came back and joined with equally embittered and unhappy workers in St. Petersburg, where economic conditions had deteriorated severely.

A pamphlet by Trotsky calling for a general strike had been widely circulated, and in January 1905, 12,000 workers at St. Petersburg's Putilov engineering works struck. When troops dispersed the strikers, support for the protestors grew. A liberal priest, Father George Gapon, hoping to prevent violence by wresting concessions from the tsar, Nicholas II, instituted an organization called the Russian Workers' Assembly.

On January 22, 1905, Gapon led 200,000 workers on a peaceful march to the tsar's sumptuous Winter Palace, carrying a petition that called for an eight-hour workday and a guaranteed minimum wage. They paraded through the streets carrying religious statues and proving their loyalty by singing "God save the tsar." The tsar was absent from the city, and the imperial troops, frightened by the sight of such a large crowd, suddenly opened fire. The deep snow in front of the Winter Palace was quickly stained with blood. Hundreds of the dying and wounded lay in the streets.

The tsar returned and called for law and order. There were widespread crackdowns. Many workers were arrested, some were executed, but none of the imperial soldiers were punished. All over the world newspaper headlines deplored the massacre.

When Trotsky learned of the events, he quickly prepared to return to his homeland. Stopping off again at Victor Adler's house in Vienna, he shaved off his beard and mustache. Natalya went on ahead to arrange for his arrival in Russia. Once again the network of revolutionary party members and sympathizers helped him on his way. At Kiev, he was hidden in an eye hospital, where his accomplices had persuaded the nurses that he really was a patient and in need of treatment. From there, he trav-

Class consciousness can only be brought to the workers from without. The history of all countries shows that the working class, exclusively by its own effort, is able to develop only trade union consciousness, i.e., the conviction that it is necessary to combine in unions, fight the employers, and strive to compel the government to pass necessary labour legislation.
—VLADIMIR LENIN
in *What Is to Be Done?*,
his 1902 landmark
contribution to Marxist theory

eled with Natalya to St. Petersburg, where the street action was at its height. There he became "Petr Petrovich," organizing workers, urging them to strike, hoping that all of this activity would lead, not to some minor concessions by the tsar, but to a bourgeois-democratic capitalist revolution that would later move on toward socialism.

When the police raided a revolutionary meeting and Natalya was arrested, Trotsky went into hiding and then fled to Finland. There, he heard that the tsar's security forces had failed to stop the forward momentum of the angry Russian workers. A general strike erupted in St. Petersburg. No streetcars ran, no banks opened, no stores did business, no machinery hummed. Even the ballet company marched in the street, waving the red banners that traditionally symbolized the revolutionary cause.

When the battleship *Potemkin* steamed into harbor at Odessa on June 15, the authorities were stunned: the brand-new vessel, pride of the tsar's navy, was flying the red flag! The *Potemkin*'s crew, tired of bad food and appalling living conditions, and full of revolutionary zeal, had mutinied, shooting, throwing overboard, or imprisoning all the ship's officers.

The rebel sailors tried to get their comrades on the other naval vessels in the harbor to join them, but the fleet's admiral quickly ordered the ships out to sea. Leaderless and confused, the revolutionary crew finally headed for a Romanian port. There they scuttled the mighty *Potemkin* and escaped into the countryside.

Meanwhile the workers of St. Petersburg took over the city. They held elections and on October 14, 1905, formed their own government, calling it the St. Petersburg *Soviet* (council) of Workers' Deputies. (Lenin regarded the soviets as "not a workers' parliament," but "a fighting organization for the attainment of definite ends." Trotsky himself considered the first meeting of the St. Petersburg soviet "more like a council of war than a parliament.")

For the next 50 days, the 26-year-old Trotsky was the leading spirit of the soviet, publishing a newspaper, organizing elections, commanding strike ac-

> *While the traditional view was that the road to the dictatorship of the proletariat led through a long period of democracy, the theory of the permanent revolution established the fact that for backward countries the road to democracy passed through the dictatorship of the proletariat.*
>
> —LEON TROTSKY
> summarizing his theory of permanent revolution, formulated during his 1906 imprisonment

The Russian fleet is annihilated by the Japanese navy during the Russo-Japanese War in 1905. The government of Nicholas II, who had been supremely confident of defeating what he called the "Japanese monkeys," was dealt a heavy blow by Russia's humiliating defeat.

tion, issuing propaganda, and arranging for the distribution of weapons. The soviet ignored the tsar's decrees and made its own laws.

The events of 1905, however, did not constitute a full-fledged revolution. On October 17, undoubtedly fearful that he would lose his throne, Nicholas II issued a manifesto promising a constitution, civil liberties, and elections. Liberals rushed to embrace the reforms, and some of the strikers also felt that an adequate victory had been won. Trotsky, however, had no illusions about the tsar's promises.

He believed that the Spentzers' dream of a "liberal" tsar could never come true. Addressing the St. Petersburg soviet, he begged them not to give up the struggle. "Now that we have put our foot on the neck of the ruling clique," he told them, "they promise us freedom. . . . Is a promise of freedom the same as freedom? Look around, citizens, has anything changed since yesterday? Are the gates of our prisons open? Have our brothers returned to their homes from the Siberian wilderness? With sword in hand we must defend freedom. The tsar's manifesto . . . see! It is only a scrap of paper." Crumpling the document in his hand, he shouted, "Today it has been given us and tomorrow it will be taken away and torn into pieces." The crowd agreed, and, for the moment, talk of giving up subsided.

Natalya, released from prison, joined Trotsky in St. Petersburg. But they were still in grave danger. This 1905 rehearsal for revolution had shaken the tsarist regime but had by no means overthrown it. St. Petersburg turned out to be the strongest point in a weak chain. When the St. Petersburg soviet published a declaration calling on people to stop paying taxes and to withdraw their bank deposits in order to damage the financial underpinnings of the tsarist order, mass arrests took place. Nicholas II had delayed moving against the St. Petersburg soviet for fear that it would be supported by workers in the heart of Russia and that troops from his own imperial army would defect. However, as liberals all over the nation demonstrated their willingness to accept his concessions, the tsar realized that he had managed to isolate Trotsky's soviet. The revolution of 1905, the dress rehearsal for the revolution that would change the face of Russia forever just 12 years

Their holy pictures and portraits of Tsar Nicholas II scattered in the bloodstained snow, terrified workers flee from the tsar's cavalry at the Winter Palace on January 22, 1905. The violent ending of the peaceful march turned many hitherto docile Russians into bitter enemies of the tsar.

later, was choked off and crushed.

All the members of the St. Petersburg soviet were rounded up. Once again Trotsky found himself in a succession of prisons. But this time there had to be a public trial. The workers of St. Petersburg and Moscow would not move on to overthrow the tsar, but neither would they become the mute slaves they had been before. There were protest strikes all over St. Petersburg. In Moscow barricades were erected and strikers fought a desperate 19-day battle with the tsar's troops.

With the eyes of the world on the arrested members of the St. Petersburg soviet, the detainees were treated as important prisoners of state. Natalya was able to visit Trotsky twice a week and he was able to smuggle out writings through his lawyer. Meanwhile, the government released 204 prisoners and decided to focus its attention on Trotsky and 14 other ringleaders.

Trotsky walked into the courtroom on September 19, 1906, for the trial of the leadership of the St. Petersburg Soviet of Workers' Deputies. His mother and father were present, his father pale, his mother tearful. The world was watching, and Trotsky was planning to give them a stellar performance.

If the tsar could get rid of the most important members of the St. Petersburg soviet, he thought, he might yet again be able to rule in peace. But if he killed the diehard activists—especially the popular Leon Trotsky—an even more threatening movement might be created.

On October 4 Leon Trotsky presented the case for the accused. In the course of a long speech about the condition of the working class in Russia, he made a comment on the nature of popular insurrection, the activity with which he had been charged and one that, under the tsarist code of justice, carried the death penalty: "A popular insurrection cannot be staged. It can only be foreseen." He went on to damn the very government that was trying him: "What we possess is not a national governmental force but a machine for mass murder."

Thousands had signed petitions for the release of the 14 defendants, who had been receiving huge

> *Without direct political aid from the European proletariat the working class of Russia will not be able to retain its power and to turn its temporary supremacy into a permanent socialist dictatorship.*
> —LEON TROTSKY

bouquets of flowers in jail. The court had to be surrounded with masses of cossacks and soldiers to prevent a rescue attempt. Because of this strong public support, the lives of Trotsky and the other 14 prisoners were spared. Instead of death, they were sentenced to enforced settlement in Siberia for life. Any escape attempts would be punished by three years of hard labor.

Once again Trotsky spent a year in a transfer prison, awaiting his deportation to Siberia. World opinion helped improve his plight. Natalya and other friends could visit him. He spent his days reading French novels and writing. Utilizing his 1905 experience to rethink the important question of how to take power away from the tsar, he formulated his theory of "permanent revolution."

This highly controversial theory would become the main core for a later work, *The Permanent Revolution*, that Trotsky was to write in 1929. The first part of the theory enraged both the Bolsheviks and the Mensheviks. It challenged the idea that capitalism—private ownership of the factories, mills, and farms, with a democratic political system— would have to come before socialism could be achieved. Trotsky proclaimed that socialism could come quickly in Russia. He said that a predominantly backward society did not have to pass through a long period of capitalist development and bourgeois democracy, and that under certain conditions, especially in a country where the *proletariat* (the working class) vastly outnumbered the bourgeoisie, progress toward socialism could be greatly accelerated.

The second and even more controversial element of the theory was that socialism could not survive if it was instituted in just one country. If the rest of the nations of the world remained capitalist, they could surround and isolate such an experiment. A socialist Russia would have to aid the spread of socialism to other countries in Europe.

On January 5, 1907, the prisoners, dressed in their gray convicts' garb, started their long trip to Siberia—this time bound for the penal colony of Obdorsk, close to the Arctic Circle and 1,000 miles from the nearest railway station. For 30 days, nearly frozen, they traveled in pairs under heavy guard, first by train and then by sleigh, through a region plagued by typhus.

Trotsky had been thinking about escape ever since receiving his sentence. He knew that if he waited until the group reached the penal colony, it would be impossible. In his left boot heel were false papers, in his right boot sole were gold coins collected by his comrades. Another prisoner, an aging doctor, taught him how to imitate the symptoms of sciatica, a nerve disorder that makes walking almost impossible. At one of the rest stops he was left behind at a hospital. There, a sympathetic land surveyor told him about an isolated escape route that would take him to a mining town in the Ural Mountains from which he could go by railway to St. Petersburg.

At midnight on February 12, 1907, concealed beneath a load of frozen hay, he began his journey. His peasant driver was a heavy drinker who often dozed off and landed the sleigh in snowdrifts. Nevertheless, they covered 430 miles in a week. Most of the time there was little sustenance to be had except for tea, the water for which they procured by boiling up snow. When they came to villages, Trotsky posed as a minor government official or as a member of a polar expedition. Again there were "friends," revolutionaries and supporters, who helped along the way. When he reached the Urals, Trotsky posed as an engineer and continued by horse to the railroad.

In Finland, where she lived alone with their baby son, Lyova, born while Trotsky was in prison, Natalya was startled to receive a cable asking her to go to the railway station in St. Petersburg. Again with the aid of revolutionary comrades, she managed to get there and bring Trotsky back to Finland, where both Martov and Lenin were also living.

Moving on to Sweden, Trotsky wrote an account of his escape that brought him enough money to travel abroad. Natalya returned to Russia with their son, expecting Trotsky to join them quickly. But Trotsky was not to set foot on Russian soil again until May 1917, a decade later.

Awaiting trial for leading the St. Petersburg *Soviet* (council) of Workers' Deputies in 1906, Trotsky rejected an escape plan proposed by some of his fellow revolutionaries. He was, he said, "attracted by the political importance of the trial ahead," and had no intention of missing it or the chance it would give him to expound his views.

4

Exile and Revolution

When Natalya returned from Russia, she reported that every policeman in the country was looking for Leon Trotsky, the daring escapee from Siberia. He would surely be picked up within five minutes if he attempted to reenter his homeland. Deciding to settle in Vienna, the Trotskys lived first in a pleasant villa. Then, running out of funds, they spent the next seven years in a tiny, three-room house in a working-class suburb of the city. There, in 1908, their second son, Sergei, was born.

Working with the Austrian Social Democratic movement was a distasteful duty for Leon Trotsky. The party members were mostly middle-class intellectuals who argued constantly and made little effort to politicize the poorer classes. Furthermore, the Viennese socialists looked down on the exiled Russian revolutionaries as backward.

In his writings during this time, Trotsky concentrated on the implications of the Russian revolution of 1905. Bolsheviks and Mensheviks alike ridiculed what he wrote in the bimonthly journal *Pravda* (*Truth*). He persisted in maintaining that the 1905 revolution was not dead but was continuing, and that it would not stop until capitalism was overthrown, first in Russia and then throughout the rest of the world. He kept busy touring the Russian

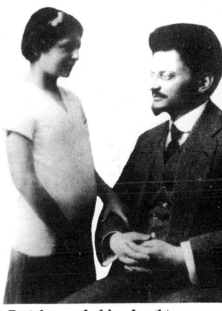

Trotsky and his daughter Nina, born during his first Siberian exile. Trotsky was to outlive all his children. Nina died of tuberculosis in the 1930s, and her sister Zina committed suicide soon afterward. Both Trotsky's sons by Natalya—Lyova and Sergei—were murdered on Stalin's orders.

Russian prisoners of war collect firewood in a German internment camp during World War I. The Russian army's morale was high at the war's outset, in 1914, but despair replaced patriotic fervor as the ill-equipped, poorly led soldiers met one crushing defeat after another. By 1915, Russian troops were surrendering at the rate of 200,000 a month.

Fiery American socialist leader Eugene Victor Debs (1855–1926) was jailed under the Espionage Act for a 1918 antiwar speech. Undiscouraged, he mounted his fifth unsuccessful campaign for the U.S. presidency, wryly predicting that he would "sweep every precinct of the penitentiary." He was pardoned and released from prison in 1921.

exile community, trying to unite the Mensheviks and the Bolsheviks, urging them to "march on common ground." His efforts, however, were futile.

Deprived of an organization and without much political work to do, Trotsky devoted more of his time to his family instead. An affectionate father, he was ahead of his time in his conduct of domestic affairs. He took over much of the child care and housework, which allowed Natalya time to pursue her art studies and her own political activities. In 1910 his parents came again to visit him, bringing his elder daughter Zina, who had never forgotten him. It was the last time he ever saw his mother. Anna Bronstein died some months later after kidney surgery in Berlin.

In 1912 Trotsky accepted a job as a journalist. He covered the Balkan Wars, which saw the combined armies of Serbia, Greece, and Bulgaria drive the Turks from the region. Trotsky was glad to get away from the bickering among Austria's Social Democrats and to inform readers of the human meaning of war at the battlefronts. This experience as a reporter was a baptism of fire for the man who would later head the Red Army, the formidable fighting machine that he would create in the wake of the Russian Revolution of 1917. He talked to injured soldiers, visited jails, and movingly described daily tragedies. When he came across evidence of Bulgarian atrocities against wounded and captured Turkish soldiers, he did not hesitate to write detailed accounts of what he had seen and heard. The Bulgarian government responded promptly, barring Trotsky from the front.

In August 1914 World War I broke out. Austria-Hungary had declared war on Serbia on July 28, and Serbia's ally, Russia, mobilized its forces along the German and Austrian frontiers on July 29. Germany then declared war on Russia on August 1 and on France, Russia's ally, on August 3. When Germany then announced that it would not respect Belgian neutrality on the march into France, Britain, Belgium's ally, declared war on Germany. Trotsky interpreted the situation as a conflict among Europe's major capitalist powers to determine which of them would become richer and more dominant. Socialists, he said, should stay out of the war. The leaders of the broad socialist organization known as the Second International of Social Democratic Parties, however, lined up with their own national rulers and told the working classes in their respective countries to fight and die as patriots. As a result, Trotsky's few friends in Vienna rapidly became his enemies.

The tremendous upsurge of patriotism and nationalism that followed the outbreak of war was very much apparent in Russia. When the tsar and tsarina appeared on a balcony of the Winter Palace, thousands of peasants fell to their knees and sang the national anthem in that very same square where just nine years earlier imperial troops had gunned down unarmed workers.

In August 1914, when the Austrian government made it a criminal offense to speak or write against the war, Trotsky and his family were forced to move to Zurich, in neutral Switzerland. There, Trotsky wrote a detailed condemnation of the war, which he entitled *The War and the International*. In this tract, he called upon Europe's workers to overthrow their governments in order to create a "republican United States of Europe, as the foundation for the United States of the World."

In November 1914 Trotsky crossed the frontier into France as a correspondent for *Kievan Thought*, a newspaper published by Russian exiles; six months later Natalya and his sons followed him. In

An improvised Russian military hospital during World War I. The conflict left at least 2 million Russian soldiers dead and 6 million wounded. The tsar's forces, not yet recovered from their devastating defeat in the war with Japan a decade before, were ill prepared to do battle with Germany's superb, modern army.

Paris, he worked with his old friend Yulii Martov on a journal called *The Voice.*

Despite all the disappointments, World War I brought Trotsky considerably closer to Lenin and the Bolsheviks, who held fast to an antiwar position similar to his own. On September 5, 1915, 38 delegates from 11 countries met in the Swiss village of Zimmerwald for an international socialist conference to debate the implications of the war. The delegates adopted the outspoken manifesto that Trotsky composed at the conference: "Workers of Europe! The war has lasted for more than a year. Millions of corpses lie on the battlefields; millions of men have been crippled for life. Europe has become a gigantic slaughterhouse. . . . In every country the capitalists who forge the gold of war profits from the blood of the people are declaring that the war is for national defense, democracy, and the liberation of oppressed nationalities. THEY LIE! In reality they are burying on the fields of devastation the liberties of their own people.

However, despite having pledged their support for the Zimmerwald Manifesto (as Trotsky's polemic came to be known), most of Trotsky's former friends came out one by one in support of the war. But the Bolsheviks did not waver, and, as a result, Trotsky's editorials pushed harder for cooperation with that particular group. Martov indignantly resigned from *Our Word* (the publication that had replaced *The Voice*), leaving Trotsky as its sole editor.

Then, once again, Trotsky and his family were forced to move on. On September 15, 1916, the French police banned *Our Word* and ordered Trotsky to leave the country. Exiled Russian revolutionaries were being hounded out of all the countries involved in the conflict because of their opposition to the war. Afraid that he would be sent back to Russia, where slave labor in Siberia awaited him, Trotsky tried desperately to get visas for Switzerland, Italy, or a Scandinavian country. But by now his opinions on the war were well known, and no neutral country wanted a confrontation with Russian diplomats. On October 30 the French police deported him to Spain.

A man of medium height, with haggard cheeks, reddish hair, and straggling red beard stepped briskly forward. His speech, first in Russian and then in German, was powerful and electrifying. I did not agree with his political attitude. . . . But his analysis of the causes of the war was brilliant, his denunciation of the ineffective Provisional Government in Russia scathing, and his presentation of the conditions that led up to the revolution illuminating.

—EMMA GOLDMAN
American socialist leader,
recalling a speech Trotsky
gave in New York in 1917

In Madrid, the Spanish capital, Trotsky stayed free for a few days, and spent his time visiting art museums. Then, on November 9, the Spanish police arrested and jailed him. Next, the police escorted him to the Spanish port city of Cadiz, where he learned that he was going to be deported to Cuba. From Cadiz he telegraphed government ministers, deputies, and liberal newspapers, urgently appealing that he be permitted to go to New York. He felt that he and his family would be safer under American democratic capitalism than in a Latin American dictatorship where he might easily be killed.

After weeks of negotiation, during which he studied English avidly, he was given permission to go to the United States with his family. They sailed on a cramped little Spanish steamer, and arrived in New York on January 13, 1917.

Again, it was the socialist movement that provided assistance to the Trotskys when they found themselves in yet another strange land. Members of America's Socialist party secured them an apartment in the district of the city known as the Bronx. The family had their first electric lights, gas range, elevator, even a garbage chute. Sergei and Lyova were especially delighted with the telephone, to which their father referred as "this mysterious instrument." At first Trotsky was impressed by the American standard of living. Later he wrote about the contradictions of America and contrasted the nation's lavish military spending with the vision of "an old man with suppurating eyes and a straggling gray beard stopping before a garbage can and fishing out a crust of bread."

Trotsky came to admire Eugene Victor Debs, an outspoken socialist leader whose fearless opposition to the authorities had earned him many months in jail, but he abhorred the elitist attitudes, private cars, and material prosperity of many of the Socialist party leaders. Trotsky immediately expressed his disillusionment with the somewhat diluted nature of American radicalism by joining the staff of *New World*, a New York-based militant Marxist weekly published by prominent Bolshevik exiles.

The family had thought that they would be in New

Workers of Europe! . . . In every country the capitalists who forge the gold of war profits from blood of the people are declaring that the war is for national defense, democracy, and the liberation of oppressed nationalities. They lie! In reality they are burying on the fields of devastation the liberties of their own peoples, together with the independence of other nations.
—LEON TROTSKY writing in 1915, expressing his opposition to World War I

York for a long time, but things had not remained quiet in Russia. All of Trotsky's predictions had come true. The liberals of Russia had proven incapable of solving the problems of the masses of people. Hoping to extend the tsar's base of support within the population at large, the government had given land grants to a select group of peasants. There did indeed develop a class of *kulaks*, or rich peasants, but the misery of the poor peasants seemed even worse by contrast, and some of them began openly to resist the tsarist regime.

As the war progressed, the conditions of the majority of the Russian working class deteriorated. A string of military defeats resulted in runaway inflation, reduced wages, and widespread strikes. Worse yet, this desperate impoverishment existed alongside the high standard of living still enjoyed by the wealthy.

The tsar had hoped for a quick victory, but his forces were no match for the Germans. The outcome of World War I was to be decided by technology and training, and backward Russia could not produce such sophisticated military hardware as that developed and deployed by the Germans. Many of the Russian soldiers had no weapons at all. An astounding 4 million of them had been slaughtered or captured in the first 10 months of fighting. German leaflets read: "Stop killing your brothers! Do not fight the tsar's war! We are workers and peasants like you—we do not want to fight you. Go home and demand the land the tsar promised you!" Thousands of Russian soldiers deserted, returning home to find nothing but bread riots, antiwar demonstrations, and strikes.

Again, the people of St. Petersburg, which had been renamed Petrograd in 1914, were in the forefront of the struggle. On February 25, 1917, women demonstrated to protest food shortages. They were joined by engineering workers who had been locked out by the factory owners to prevent a sitdown strike. By the next morning, 200,000 people were on strike, marching in the streets against the tsar and the war.

By Saturday, February 27, a general strike was

Tsar Nicholas II entertains Germany's Kaiser Wilhelm II (1859–1941) aboard his royal yacht. The rulers—who were cousins—maintained a cordial relationship until 1914, when they led their respective nations to war against each other.

in effect. Nothing moved in the city. The tsar issued new orders: troops were to fire on any crowd refusing to disperse. On Sunday, February 28, a group of demonstrators on one bank of the Catherine Canal was fired upon by soldiers stationed along the opposite bank. Another contingent of soldiers passing along the bank occupied by the crowd became enraged at the sight of their comrades shooting unarmed men, women, and children. They fired back. The revolt within the tsar's army had begun.

That night, troops loyal to the tsar captured the rebels in their barracks, but by now the engine of revolution was rolling fast. In another nearby barracks, the soldiers who had fired on the demonstrators that same afternoon decided that they would no longer take part in such slaughter. Many of them joined the workers, bringing their guns along with them.

The lessons of 1905 had not been forgotten. Throughout March 1917 a soviet was operating in Petrograd. Its provisional executive committee called for elections. The soldiers who had joined the workers' cause came to the meeting of the soviet and gave their own accounts of the recent incidents. The workers in the hall stamped and roared their approval, and, by a unanimous vote, the Petrograd Soviet of Workers' Deputies was renamed the Petrograd Soviet of Workers' and Soldiers' Deputies.

At the Winter Palace, liberal members of the State *Duma*, or legislative assembly, were busy convincing the tsar that he would have to abdicate or they would all lose everything. By March 2, all government ministers in Petrograd were under "people's" arrest. That same day, Tsar Nicholas II abdicated, ending the 300-year-old Romanov dynasty. Soldiers' deputies controlled the streets, hunting down members of the tsar's secret police and freeing all political prisoners. Also on March 2, a new constitutional body, the Provisional Government, was formed, and received the support of both the Mensheviks, who were now allied with the Social-Revolutionaries, and the Bolsheviks, most of whom were still in exile or hiding. A liberal noble, Prince Georgy Lvov, led the

Trotsky had high hopes that Germany's Marxist movement, led by "Red Rosa" Luxemburg (1870–1919) and Karl Liebknecht (1871–1919), would succeed in establishing communism in Germany. The German revolution, however, suffered a fatal blow when Luxemburg and Liebknecht were murdered following their party's attempted takeover of Berlin in 1919.

council of ministers. Alexander Kerensky, a 35-year-old Social-Revolutionary, was appointed minister of justice.

From the point of view of the soldiers and workers, however, not enough had changed. For one thing, the Provisional Government was determined to keep Russia in the war. On April 3, following a long train ride from Switzerland, Lenin arrived at the Finland Station in Petrograd.

At a conference the following day, Lenin presented his views to the assembled Petrograd soviet. He said that they should not count on the "capitalists" in the Provisional Government. The revolution must continue on to socialism, he declared, or nothing would change. Lenin had thus, much to the dismay of many of the Bolsheviks, Mensheviks, and various other social democrats present, seemingly endorsed Trotsky's theory of permanent revolution.

Meanwhile, in New York, news of the disturbances in Petrograd reached the Trotskys. On February 28, two days before the abdication of Tsar Nicholas II, Trotsky wrote: "We are the witnesses of the beginning of the second Russian revolution. Let us hope that many of us will be participants."

Trotsky's sons, Lyova and Sergei, had become real New Yorkers. They had learned English, and Natalya had made American friends and grown to love the city's cultural attractions. Suddenly, however, the only important goal for Trotsky and Natalya was to return to Russia. The Provisional Government voted to permit all political exiles to reenter the country. New York friends held a fundraising rally to pay for the Trotskys' passage, and on March 27 the jubilant family sailed from New York aboard a Norwegian freighter on the first leg of a tortuous journey back to Russia—and revolution!

Initially, it seemed that the Trotskys would never reach Russia. After only a few days at sea, the ship stopped at Halifax, a port in the Canadian province of Nova Scotia. There, the British police arrested Trotsky as a person dangerous to the Allied war effort.

Trotsky found himself in the company of over 800 German prisoners of war, to whom he immediately

We appeal to the vigilance and courage of the workers, soldiers and peasants of all Russia. Petrograd is in danger! The Revolution is in danger! The nation is in danger. The government aggravates this danger. The ruling parties help it. Only the people themselves can save the country. We turn to the people. All power to the Soviets. All the land to the People!

—LEON TROTSKY denouncing the Provisional Government and calling for a Bolshevik revolution, October 7, 1917

Terrified St. Petersburg protesters flee from rooftop machine-gun fire in July 1917. Popular demonstrations against the war and the Provisional Government had begun peacefully, but escalated into bloody street-fighting when anarchists and ultraradical sailors from the Kronstadt naval fortress joined the volatile crowds.

began to make revolutionary speeches. He shunned the German officers and insisted on doing camp chores alongside the ordinary soldiers.

On April 16 Trotsky was released. The Petrograd soviet had put pressure on Prince Lvov, and since Russia was still allied with Great Britain, an agreement was reached. The German officers too, fearing that their troops would become revolutionaries if Trotsky remained in their midst, urged the prison officials to set the rabble-rouser free.

Once again the Trotskys headed toward the revolution, first to Finland aboard a Danish vessel and then by train to Petrograd. On May 4, 1917, one month after Lenin's return, Leon Trotsky arrived at the railroad station and was carried triumphantly on the shoulders of a welcoming crowd.

Trotsky was immediately escorted to the Tauride Palace, where the Petrograd soviet awaited him. All along the route he could hardly believe the joyous sight of soldiers marching with red flags and singing revolutionary songs.

A room was found for the family, and Trotsky immediately plunged into the task of convincing the Petrograd soviet that the revolution had to be carried forward to socialism. He dashed from one area of the city to another, speaking day and night at mass meetings in schools, theaters, factories, and squares. He barely slept or saw Natalya and the boys.

Between May and October of 1917 an intense struggle went on inside the Petrograd soviet between moderate socialists and the Bolsheviks. Along with his shocking demand that the soviet cease to support the coalition government, Lenin called for Russia's immediate withdrawal from the war. Un-

The proletariat needs state power, the centralized organization of force, the organization of violence, both to crush the resistance of the exploiters and to lead the enormous mass of the population—the peasantry, the petty bourgeoisie, the semiproletarians in the work of organizing a socialist economy.
—VLADIMIR LENIN
in *The State and Revolution*,
September 1917

Russian Prime Minister Alexander Kerensky (1881–1970) supported liberal political reforms, but the people wanted food and peace, neither of which his Provisional Government could supply. After the relatively bloodless coup in which he was overthrown in 1917, Kerensky fled to Paris, where he lived until he moved to the United States in 1940.

able to change the minds of the Mensheviks, Trotsky and his followers joined the Bolsheviks. His 14-year feud with Lenin was over.

But the debates inside the soviet had little impact on the hunger and misery then afflicting the citizens of Petrograd. After the initial flush of victory that followed the abdication of the tsar, people had expected miraculous changes. Instead, conditions continued to be grim. "Land, bread, and peace," the slogan that had helped bring about the downfall of the tsar, now seemed little more than empty words. The war dragged on, bread lines grew longer, and robberies became rampant. Life did not seem much different under the new, "democratic" government.

In July 1917 a spontaneous mass uprising took place in Petrograd. Twenty thousand armed sailors stationed on the naval fortress at Kronstadt joined in. The Bolsheviks considered these actions premature and opposed them, but the Provisional Government nevertheless accused the Bolsheviks of inciting the people to riot. After days of street fighting, the Menshevik executive committee of the Petrograd soviet sent in the hated cossacks and disarmed the workers.

Fearful that another uprising might succeed, Kerensky, who was now the leader of the Provisional Government, decided to move against the Bolsheviks. Lenin, accused of being a German spy, donned a wig, shaved his beard, and went into hiding. Trotsky was arrested again and thrown into Kresty prison, one of the many jails where he had spent dismal days in his youth.

Meanwhile, popular distrust of the Provisional Government was increasing. In early September, rising public pressure forced Kerensky to release Trotsky on bail. A few days later, he was elected president of the Petrograd soviet. Throughout the country, Bolsheviks won elections to lead the other soviets that had been formed as the revolution spread.

On October 24, 1917, Lenin came out of hiding and returned to Petrograd for a secret meeting of the central committee of the Bolshevik party. Together, he and Trotsky persuaded the majority of the deputies to vote for immediate seizure of power.

Again, Trotsky took to the streets to convince the Petrograd workers. He seemed to be everywhere at once. Within days, virtually every worker and soldier in the city either knew of Trotsky or had listened to him speak.

In the early hours of October 25, 1917, the military-revolutionary committee of the Petrograd soviet, led by the 37-year-old Leon Trotsky, launched a successful insurrection. In less than 11 hours, thousands of insurgents seized and occupied the railway stations, post offices, telegraph offices, and banks. At mid-day Trotsky was able to inform the soviet that the revolutionaries had taken over the capital. Kerensky had fled the city under the protection of a foreign embassy, some ministers in the Provisional Government had been arrested, and the few remaining counterrevolutionary elements in Petrograd were holed up in the Winter Palace.

Later that same day, as Bolshevik troops stormed the Winter Palace, the workers', sailors', and soldiers' deputies, still dressed in their ragged clothes and dirty and tired from the long day of struggle in the streets, crowded into the marble halls of the Smolny Institute—formerly a fashionable school for the daughters of the Russian nobility—to attend the Second All-Russian Congress of Soviets. Lenin mounted a podium and told the wildly cheering deputies: "We shall now proceed to construct the socialist order!"

It seemed that Trotsky spoke everywhere simultaneously. Every worker and soldier of Petrograd knew him and listened to him. His influence on the masses and leaders alike was overwhelming. He was the central figure of those days, and the chief hero of this remarkable chapter of history.
—N. SUKHANOV
leading Menshevik, praising Trotsky's skill in mustering support for the Bolshevik overthrow of the Provisional Government

Lenin addresses the Second All-Russian Congress of Soviets in October 1917. Greeted with roars of approval, his manifesto promised to transfer land to the peasants, democratize the army, and put workers in charge of industry.

5

The Dream Defended

As their deputies cheered Lenin and Trotsky, the workers and soldiers talked late into the night about the new Russia that had just been born. Not only would there be genuine democracy for everyone, they said, there would be equality. No more would the rich ride in luxury through the streets past unemployed beggars. No more would the workers have to be satisfied with bread and cabbage while their employers ate fresh meat and drank good vodka. In a few years, the new state would be building homes to replace the shacks, and machinery to help the peasants produce more food.

Trotsky had predicted that without socialist revolutions in the rest of Europe, the dream of a Russian workers' paradise would be trampled. The whole capitalist world would move in to prevent the socialist ideal from becoming a reality. He could not have known, though, that from the ruins the invaders would leave in their wake, power-hungry men would rise up; that he, Leon Trotsky, would again be a man without a country, this time despised by his former comrades and hunted over the face of the earth.

The man who would be the chief author of the nightmare sat at the Smolny Institute cheering with the others. His name was Joseph Stalin, and in just a few years he would become Trotsky's most implacable enemy.

Published during Russia's 1918–21 civil war, a propaganda poster shows a valiant Trotsky slaying a top-hatted dragon, which represents the capitalist-inspired counterrevolution. All such heroic representations of the communist leader disappeared from the Soviet Union after his banishment by Stalin.

Show me another man who could organize almost a model army in a single year.
—VLADIMIR LENIN
praising Trotsky's skill as people's commissar for war

A Red Army woman recruit drills during the civil war that followed the revolution. As commissar of war in 1918, Trotsky faced the almost impossible job of organizing the infant Soviet state's defenses against both foreign invaders and Russian counterrevolutionaries. By 1920, however, he had created what Lenin called "an almost model army."

Red Army troops listen to an impassioned speech by Trotsky in 1919. "We will not give up our beloved Petrograd, comrades!" he shouted. "It is the base and dishonest England of the stock exchange manipulators that is fighting us. The England of labor and the people is with us!"

Even before the celebration and the wild, festive drinking parties had ended, the revolutionary leaders were faced with a vast number of problems. Defeated in the elections, the Mensheviks still demanded an equal role in the new government. When this was refused, Trotsky's old friend Martov led them in a walkout. Faced with hostile Mensheviks and the threat of sabotage by diehard supporters of the tsar, the Bolsheviks also had to resolve the pressing issue of the war.

The new Bolshevik government had promised to end Russian participation in the conflict by signing a separate peace treaty with Germany. After all, the interests of tsarist Russia were no longer the interests of the new, socialist state. First, Trotsky called on all the participants in the war to negotiate a truce. Not only were his pleas totally ignored, but the Allied leaders spread incredible stories that Lenin and Trotsky were German spies.

Following this rebuff, the Bolshevik leaders gave urgent and serious consideration to the question of how peace might best be achieved. Critical differences of opinion quickly emerged—differences that threatened to divide the party at a time when unity was vital. By the end of 1917, the Germans were in possession of large areas of Russian territory. Lenin wanted immediate peace, no matter what the territorial loss, but Trotsky wanted to stall negotiations with the representatives of Germany's *Kaiser* (emperor) Wilhelm II, in the hope that a revolution would take place in Germany. The Bolshevik party, still following the democratic model of the soviets, opened the debate to the public. Both sides of the issue were set forth in the pages of *Pravda*, provoking heated and widespread discussion.

At the end of November 1917, his position victorious, Trotsky, now people's commissar for foreign affairs, went to negotiate with the Germans in the Polish city of Brest-Litovsk, where he duly managed to secure a 17-day truce. He hoped that, in this brief period, the German leftists would stage a successful revolution and that he would then be negotiating with a new, socialist government of Germany.

> *One wondered if a country so despairing, so devastated, had enough sap left in it to support a new regime and preserve its independence. There was no food. There was no army. The railways were completely disorganized. The machinery of state was just beginning to take shape. Conspiracies were being hatched everywhere.*
> —LEON TROTSKY
> describing the problems facing the Bolshevik leadership in 1918

The tsar and tsarina of Russia, Nicholas II and Alexandra, and their five children. Anastasia, the daughter believed by some to have survived the massacre of her family in 1918, is third from the right.

White Russian (anti-Bolshevik) soldiers prepare for a Bolshevik attack. By the end of 1918, the new Soviet government was under siege by 180,000 Allied troops and a 300,000-man force armed and financed by Britain, the United States, France, and other former allies of Russia.

'In what do your tactics differ from the tactics of Tsarism?' we are asked by the high priests of Liberalism. . . . You do not understand this, holy men? We shall explain to you. The gendarmerie of Tsarism throttled the workers who were fighting for the socialist order. Our Extraordinary Commissions shoot landlords, capitalists, and generals who are striving to restore the capitalist order.

—LEON TROTSKY
in *Terrorism and Communism*

When the Russian delegates returned to Brest-Litovsk on December 25 for continued negotiations, Trotsky spoke passionately to General Max Hoffmann, head of the German delegation and supreme commander of German forces on the Russian front: "What in our conduct surprises and repels other governments is that we do not arrest strikers but capitalists who lock out workers; that we do not shoot peasants who demand land, but arrest landlords and officers who try to shoot peasants." Hoffmann was not impressed. The Germans held the winning card—vast tracts of captured Russian territory.

In February 1918 the Germans launched a new offensive, overruning even more Russian territory. Again, Trotsky urged the Allies to negotiate a peace, but it was clear that the Allies preferred to see Germany destroy the Bolsheviks. With no sign of the German revolutionaries stepping up their struggle for power, the Bolshevik central committee endorsed Lenin's proposal that peace be secured by any means necessary. On March 3, 1918, a sad and defeated Trotsky signed a separate peace with Germany.

That spring and summer it looked as though the beleaguered Russian Revolution would die in its infancy. The country was in ruins. Transportation had virtually ground to a halt and there was barely enough food for survival. There were conspiracies everywhere, but the government of the Russian Soviet Republic did not even have an army. Trotsky was now living with Natalya and their two sons in the Kremlin, the official government building in Moscow. Once again he had little time for his family or for sleep. There seemed to be no end to the enemies of the revolution.

Particularly frightening to the revolutionary leaders was the possibility that the tsar might be set free and reestablished on the throne. The imperial family and their servants were in Ekaterinburg, a city in the Ural Mountains, where they had been exiled for safety by the Provisional Government. On July 16, 1918, Nicholas, his wife, Alexandra, his 14-year-old son, and his four young daughters, were herded into a cellar and shot by Bolshevik troops. The killings shocked the entire world. (Ten years later, a woman named Anastasia Tschaikovsky claimed that she was the tsar's youngest daughter, the Grand Duchess Anastasia, and that she had been rescued by soldiers after her family's murder. Although her story caused worldwide public interest, and became the subject of books, plays, and movies, she died without being able to prove its accuracy.)

In the diary that he wrote many years later, Trotsky, noting that some "liberal" party members had tried to blame the massacre of the imperial family on an isolated group of local Bolsheviks, confirmed that it was in fact carried out on the specific orders of Lenin. Trotsky also defended those orders. "The execution of the tsar's family," he wrote, "was needed not only in order to frighten, horrify, and dishearten the enemy, but also in order to shake up our own ranks, to show them that there was no turning back, that ahead lay either complete victory or complete ruin."

The entry about the necessity of killing the Romanov family appears in Trotsky's diary among many heartbroken expressions of concern about his son Sergei, who had by then (1935) been arrested by Stalin simply because he was Trotsky's son. It seemed not to occur to Trotsky that the injustice of Stalin's treatment of the innocent Sergei in any way paralleled Lenin's treatment of the tsar's innocent children.

After the tsar's death, many of his generals fled the country, but those who stayed were not imprisoned. The new revolutionary government had wanted to show the world that, despite its execution of the tsar, it was not violent or vengeful. These same generals, calling themselves the Whites, were openly preparing an attack on the Bolshevik government. The Allied powers, angered by the Bolshevik government's decision to negotiate a separate peace, not only gave money and arms to the Whites but also decided to intervene directly to crush the world's first socialist state. Over 50,000 Allied soldiers—British, American, Italian, Serbian,

Trotsky addresses troops from atop his armored train, which was his home for over two years. "My own personal life was inseparably bound up with the life of that train," he wrote in his memoirs. "The train, on the other hand, was inseparably bound up with the life of the Red Army."

We believe that a strong full-blooded movement is unthinkable without controversy—only in a cemetery can total identity of opinions be achieved.
—JOSEPH STALIN

Red Army soldiers with slaughtered White troops. Recognizing the growing sympathy of their own people—both at home and at the front—with the embattled Russian revolutionaries, the Allies began pulling their armies out of Russia in 1919; withdrawal of Allied support fatally weakened the White cause, which, by 1920, was lost.

Czech, French, Polish, and Japanese—were sent to join the crusade to overthrow the revolution.

Trotsky, who had proven himself a military genius during the October uprising, was given the herculean task of turning a vast mass of undisciplined military units into an army strong enough to defend the revolution. He left the safety of his Kremlin home and for three years, from 1918 to 1921, became a symbol of Soviet resistance to Allied intervention. He traveled from one battlefield to another in an armored train equipped with a printing press, telegraph, radio, electric power stations, a bath, a garage, and even a library. Trotsky became an almost legendary figure. Discouraged Russians would see him jumping from his train in a long cavalryman's cloak and soldier's hat, mount a horse, and ride out to persuade peasants to join the Red Army, the fighting force that he had first begun to build early in 1918 and which would have 5 million men under arms by 1920.

Behind the scenes, Joseph Stalin sat on the Revolutionary War Council and whispered malicious rumors in Lenin's ear about Trotsky's military tactics. The Stalin-Trotsky feud was to become historic, but from 1918 to 1921 Trotsky's reputation was so great that it could not be damaged. When British-armed troops from Estonia and Latvia (formerly provinces of the Russian Empire) threatened

> *I confess I felt as if I were being led to the torture chamber. Being with strange and alien people always had aroused my fears; it did especially on this occasion.*
>
> —LEON TROTSKY
> recalling how he felt while negotiating an armistice with Germany at Brest-Litovsk in December 1917

68

Petrograd, Stalin advised Lenin to give up the city and rush his troops to the defense of Moscow. Trotsky's train was many miles away, but he hurried back to the Kremlin and opposed the defeatist plan. After he had persuaded Lenin to give him a chance to save the ancient city, he raced on to Petrograd.

British tanks were in the suburbs and the British navy was ready to shell the city. It seemed certain that Petrograd would fall. Trotsky's train arrived on October 26, 1919, his 40th birthday and the second anniversary of the Russian Revolution. Determined to turn every citizen of Petrograd into a committed combatant, Trotsky made fiery speeches on street corners, in taverns, factories, and mills, mesmerizing his audiences.

Men, women, and children dug trenches and fortified their homes, gardens, and backyards. Women were taught to fire machine guns. Trotsky himself was often to be found in the thick of the fighting. Workers attacked tanks and kept coming in waves even as lines were mown down. Within a week of Trotsky's arrival the people of Petrograd had beaten back the enemy and taken the offensive.

Convinced, as always, that socialism could never succeed if it were limited to one country, Trotsky found time to keep attempting to spread the revolution even while he led battles to ward off the immediate danger. In Germany, what appeared to be

White Russian troops assemble around the bodies of newly killed Bolshevik soldiers. Both Whites and Reds committed atrocities during Russia's brutal civil war. In 1919, White forces killed over 100,000 Jews.

Trotsky presides over a 1921 session of the Third International, which he created in 1919. Trotsky had hoped that widespread revolutions would follow World War I, but he was doomed to disappointment. The war had taken its toll, and Europe's workers had neither the strength nor the will to rise in revolt.

the long-awaited German revolution began in December 1918. In January 1919, however, when social revolution turned into armed opposition to the government, the insurrection was crushed and its leaders, Karl Liebknecht and Rosa Luxemburg, were assassinated by rightists.

Hoping that an international meeting of communist parties would speed up revolutions in other countries, Lenin called a conference to found the Third International, or Comintern, an organization dedicated to the overthrow of capitalism throughout the world. (The previous Internationals had existed between 1864 and 1876 and 1889 and 1914.) The conference was held in Moscow in 1919, at the height of the Russian civil war. Trotsky drafted a manifesto calling for international revolution, which was unanimously endorsed by the 35 delegates eligible to vote out of the 50 who attended.

For a while it seemed that the Allied attacks would not cease until Russia had bled to death. Early in 1920 Trotsky's train roared to the Ukraine, where Polish troops were invading. Again the Red Army was victorious, beating back the Polish soldiers right to their own borders. Lenin believed that if the Russian troops pushed the Polish army all the way to Warsaw, the Polish capital, the Polish people would overthrow their leaders and welcome the Russians. Trotsky warned him that the people of Poland

Now we are asked to give up our victory, to come to an agreement. With whom? You are wretched, disunited individuals; you are bankrupts. Your part is over. Go to the place where you belong from now on—the dustbin of history.
—LEON TROTSKY
responding to Menshevik pleas for a coalition government following the Bolshevik uprising

would have to make their own revolution. They would fight against any invaders, just as the people of Petrograd had done. Trotsky's assessment of the situation soon turned out to have been extremely accurate. Instead of taking Warsaw, the Russians lost a bloody battle at its gates and were then driven back more than 200 miles.

At last, after three long years, the governments of the Western democracies that were hostile to the Bolsheviks, faced with the successes gained by the Red Army and coming under mounting criticism from liberals and trade unionists at home, abandoned their policies of intervention. Trotsky's famous train was dismantled and, once again, he went home to his family.

> *The revolution has to be safeguarded no matter what the price.*
> —VLADIMIR LENIN
> explaining the decision to accept the peace terms dictated by the Germans at Brest-Litovsk in 1918

Deutschlands ideale Zukunft unter der Herrschaft des Bolschewisten

Typical of the anti-Marxist literature that flooded Germany in 1919, this poster shows a bearded revolutionary spreading darkness and destruction over the land. The caption reads: "Germany's ideal future under the rule of the Bolsheviks." After the assassination of its major leaders in 1919, the German revolution, too, was dead.

6

The Dream Destroyed

The new Bolshevik government had not been toppled, but its enemies knew that fighting off the Whites and the Allies had eroded the party's capacity to provide the effective leadership that would be required if Russia was to recover from the ravages of war and proceed toward socialism. A generation of politically conscious workers had been decimated. Aside from the war dead, over 9 million Russians had perished from cold, starvation, and disease. The economy lay in ruins. Industry had been virtually destroyed and agriculture barely existed.

During the civil war the Bolsheviks had met the economic emergency by imposing a policy called War Communism. As enemies attacked from all sides, tighter state controls had taken the place of democratic decision-making by the soviets. To prevent counterrevolution and sabotage, the state police, or Cheka, was created. It grew very strong. The Russian Socialist Federal Soviet Republic and the other soviet socialist republics that would unite as the Union of Soviet Socialist Republics in 1923 had been militarized, with the Bolshevik party as the general staff.

A Siberian peasant gets a close haircut during the epidemic of typhus—an often fatal disease transmitted by lice and fleas—that swept Russia in the early 1920s. David Bronstein, Trotsky's father, was among the epidemic's victims. After a happy, post-civil war reunion with his son, he died of the disease in 1922.

Trotsky's appearance—as suggested by this snapshot of a mild man in his mid-40s, wearing a favorite old leather jacket—belied his intense and highly charged personality. Trotsky was happiest when engaged in revolutionary dialogue, fiery speechmaking, or violent action.

Lenin records a speech addressed to the Soviet people. The teachings of Lenin, who is regarded as the architect of the Soviet state, were to be perverted by his successor, Joseph Stalin (1879–1953), who made sure that Lenin's last message—in which he called Stalin's brutal style "intolerable in a secretary general [of the Communist party]"—was never made public.

Supposedly these had been temporary measures, but it proved difficult to dismantle the powerful, repressive apparatus and reestablish democracy. In 1920 Trotsky submitted a proposal to relax economic restrictions, but it was defeated by Lenin and the rest of the central committee. Next, Trotsky proposed a new labor program to solve the economic crisis. He wanted to see "everybody working top-speed." He insisted that Russia could "skip whole centuries of economic development." By this time, however, the workers were so exhausted that even Trotsky's speeches failed to move them.

In March 1921 the soviet representing the sailors at the Kronstadt naval base, near Petrograd, initiated a revolt against the Bolshevik government. Some of the rebels were the same sailors who had been involved in the storming of the Winter Palace. Many were the sons of peasants. They published their demands, all of which were part of the basic program of the Russian Revolution itself: an end to government confiscation of grain, reestablishment of the secret ballot, freedom of speech and of the press for all revolutionary groups, and freedom for trade unions.

The Bolshevik leaders, still suspicious of everyone after the recent invasion by the Western nations, accused the sailors of being in league with the Whites. Before the spring thaw, General Mikhail Tukhachevsky, a hero of the revolution, led units loyal to the Bolsheviks over the ice to the island of Kronstadt to crush the sailors' mutiny.

A terrible, bloody battle ensued, and the Kronstadt sailors were annihilated. Trotsky's subsequent silence concerning this incident lost him many friends—friends he would sorely need in the years ahead.

As the outnumbered Kronstadt sailors were fighting to the last man, the 10th party congress opened in Moscow. At this congress Lenin proposed a plan he called the New Economic Policy, or NEP. He called for the abolition of War Communism, prohibition of grain seizures, and the right of peasants to sell some of their produce on the open market. Had it been announced a few weeks earlier, NEP might

Anarchist Emma Goldman (1869–1940) at a 1921 Moscow conference. Deported from the United States in 1919 for her antidraft activities, Goldman was at first a passionate defender of the Russian Revolution of 1917. Like many Western sympathizers, however, she was profoundly disillusioned by the repressive climate of post-revolutionary Russia.

have prevented the uprising of the Kronstadt sailors, but it had come too late.

NEP's immediate result was an increase in the food available to the cities, as peasants began marketing their products. Its longer-term results, however, were disastrous. The kulaks grew more prosperous, but poorer peasants could not compete.

Trotsky had not spoken out on Kronstadt and had supported the New Economic Policy. Now, at the 10th congress, he made another decision that was to have even more unfortunate results. He voted for the banning of opposition parties and factions, believing, as did many other Bolsheviks, that the suspension of democracy was temporary, a way of preventing the government from falling into the wrong hands.

> *Idealists and pacifists always accused the revolution of 'excesses.' But the main point is that 'excesses' flow from the very nature of revolution which in itself is but an excess of history. Whoever so desires may on this basis reject revolution in general. I do not. In this sense I carry full responsibility for the suppression of the Kronstadt rebellion.*
> —LEON TROTSKY referring to the brutal suppression of the 1921 Kronstadt garrison uprising

Victims of the famine that stalked Russia after the civil war, a peasant family takes to the road in search of food. Thousands of peasants starved to death between 1919 and 1921; in the cities, hungry workers carried banners reading, "Down with Lenin and horseflesh. Give us the tsar and pork."

The 11th party congress, held in March 1922, was the last one that Lenin attended. Since Lenin trusted Stalin to carry out decisions efficiently if not imaginatively, the central committee elected Stalin general secretary of the party. Two months later, Lenin lay bedridden, paralyzed by a stroke. Party leadership passed to a triumvirate composed of Comintern chief Grigory Zinoviev, Lev Kamenev—who was Trotsky's brother-in-law—and Joseph Stalin.

Not sensing the danger, Trotsky made no effort to become part of the top leadership. He had always hated bureaucratic posts, and much preferred active work to a desk job. He disliked the heavy drinking, vicious invective, and unscrupulous power-broking that had come to characterize life inside the Bolshevik party. Furthermore, he was very tired and often ill. The hard years had taken a toll on his health. With the war over, his position as chairman of the Military Revolutionary Council was strictly honorary. To Stalin's delight, the decision-making powers of his arch rival had been sharply curtailed.

Stalin had always considered Trotsky his main competition. They were close in age, but Trotsky was a better writer, speaker, and military leader. Furthermore, he was clearly Lenin's favorite. Now, with Trotsky's popularity in decline, Stalin pushed his own supporters into leadership posts and gained control over the party.

Lenin, slowly recovering, began to realize what was happening. He started to write notes for the next party congress: "Our workers' state is deformed—the weight of bureaucracy is too great—the division between Trotsky and Stalin spells disaster." In fact, Lenin planned to remove Stalin as general secretary at the 12th party congress in March 1923, but in December 1922 he suffered another stroke.

With his wife's help, Lenin wrote a last will and testament warning about the "vast power" Stalin had taken in his hands—"a machine borrowed from tsarism." Too ill to attend the congress and unwill-

Lenin is no more. . . . These words fall upon our minds as heavily as a giant rock falls into the sea. Can one believe it? Can one make peace with this?
—LEON TROTSKY
tribute to the recently deceased Lenin, cabled to the Kremlin on January 25, 1924

Collective farmers review Moscow's newest rulings on their economic rights. Although Lenin's New Economic Policy (NEP) was aimed at improving the lot of Russia's beleaguered peasants, the plan actually aided only the profit-hungry kulaks (prosperous peasants).

ing to direct a political battle from his bed, he waited to recover.

In October 1923 a struggle for party democracy began. Trotsky drew up a petition which he asked the central committee to consider passing on to all party branches. Signed by 46 party members, it charged Stalin with abuse of power and called for his removal as general secretary. The signatories also demanded better economic planning, freedom of criticism, and an emergency party conference. Zinoviev wanted Stalin to arrest Trotsky on the spot, but Stalin told him that Trotsky was still too popular. Instead, the petition was kept secret, Trotsky was censured (officially criticized), and the 46 dissident party members were informed that they had violated the 1921 ban on factions—the ban that Trotsky himself had supported.

From then on, Trotsky led the opposition and Stalin led the bureaucracy. On January 18, 1924, Trotsky, still in poor health, decided to take a vacation at a Black Sea resort. At a stopover on the trip, he received a telegram from Stalin. Lenin had died on January 21. Trotsky was advised to continue with his trip because, said Stalin, he could not possibly make it back in time for the funeral on January 22.

Actually, however, Stalin had scheduled the funeral for January 27. With Trotsky absent, Stalin was able to move even further into the public eye and make himself the center of the whole ceremony.

Immediately after the funeral, Stalin launched a full-scale campaign against Trotsky and everyone who embraced his ideas. Support of Trotsky's pro-democracy faction quickly came to mean loss of jobs and housing.

Lenin's widow, Krupskaya, let it be known that she was angered by the "monstrous campaign of persecution." But Stalin had far more power than those who opposed him, and he was moving very quickly to consolidate his position.

Krupskaya had one more card to play. She was in possession of the testament in which Lenin had urged the removal of Stalin as general secretary. She demanded that it be read to the next party congress.

> *Stalin is too rude, and this fault, entirely supportable in relations among us communists, becomes insupportable in the office of a general secretary. Therefore, I propose to the comrades to find a way to remove Stalin from the position and appoint to it another man who in all respects differs from Stalin.*
>
> —VLADIMIR LENIN
> in the postscript to his last
> will and testament,
> January 4, 1924

Zinoviev, Kamenev, and Stalin all refused and the central committee concurred by a 40 to 10 vote. Not wanting to appear to be seeking personal power, Trotsky abstained from voting.

Despite Trotsky's silence, Stalin escalated his campaign of vilification. In May 1924 the 13th party congress condemned the prodemocracy faction in general and Trotsky in particular. Trotsky was removed from his post as people's commissar for war. The following year the central committee removed him from the Military Revolutionary Council and prohibited him from making public speeches. The anti-Trotsky campaign spread all over the country.

At the 14th party congress, convened in December 1925 and during which the Russian Communist party changed its name to the "All-Union Communist party (Bolsheviks)," Stalin decided that the time was ripe to proclaim his theory of socialism in one country. Zinoviev and Kamenev, who had supported Stalin all along on most issues, found this particular position impossible to accept and believed that Stalin's experiment, if implemented, would prove disastrous. Belatedly, they told the congress about Lenin's last testament. They were called liars and traitors. Krupskaya demanded a free debate and was rudely silenced.

At first Trotsky refused to join forces with Zinoviev and his supporters. He had long ago written them off as despicable weaklings. In April 1926, however, with his own forces growing weaker every day, Trotsky met with Zinoviev and Kamenev in private, following a meeting of the central committee at which the three of them had, somewhat unexpectedly, discovered that there were certain issues upon which they could reach agreement. Trotsky listened to their admissions of guilt and learned the full and shocking truth. They had plotted against him with Stalin, helped to fabricate lies, and had even gone along with a failed plan to ambush and murder him. Reluctantly, Trotsky admitted them to the ranks of what was to become known as the Joint Opposition. The last great fight within the party was about to take place and Trotsky needed all the help he could get.

> *My practical work was performed under impossible conditions. It is no exaggeration to say that much of the creative activity of Stalin and his assistant Molotov was devoted to organizing direct sabotage around me.*
> —LEON TROTSKY describing the problems he faced as a member of the Supreme Economic Council, to which he was appointed in May 1925

Trotsky leaves in 1928 for his third Siberian exile, this time in remote Alma-Ata. Characteristically making the best of a bad situation, Trotsky wrote friends from Siberia about the pleasures of hunting trips with his son Lyova, "sleeping in the open air, eating mutton cooked in a pail under the sky."

With the addition of Zinoviev's supporters, the Joint Opposition may have had as many as 8,000 members inside the party in 1927. This was a very small minority indeed, since total party membership at that time is now estimated to have stood at 1 million. They operated under tremendous handicaps. Outlawed by the party itself, they had to meet secretly. Stalin, of course, had the whole party apparatus and press at his disposal. The Joint Opposition could barely manage to circulate its program.

On November 14 the central committee expelled Trotsky and Zinoviev from the party. Other prominent members of the Joint Opposition were expelled from the central committee.

Trotsky was alone when Stalin's next order came. For the third time in his life, he was to be exiled to Siberia. It was a painful and terrible blow. This time the order came not from the tsarist regime but from the revolutionary government that he had helped create. His place of exile was to be Alma-Ata, a city near the Chinese border, 2,500 miles from Moscow.

But Stalin had not anticipated Trotsky's tenacity. Just as he had done years before when he was exiled by the tsar, Trotsky smuggled articles and letters

Do you think that Stalin is now considering how to reply to your arguments? You are mistaken. He is thinking how to destroy you, to slander you, to trump up a military conspiracy, and then, when the ground has been prepared, to perpetrate a terroristic act.
—LEV B. KAMENEV
prominent Bolshevik and
opponent of Stalin
speaking to Trotsky in 1926

out to Moscow, this time crusading against the Stalinist betrayal of the principles that had inspired the Russian Revolution. When the secret police warned him that he would face banishment if he failed to stop his attacks on Stalin, Trotsky declared: "We know our duty and we will do it to the end." He appealed to the Comintern, but Stalin, now the organization's absolute master, announced that its activities were to be suspended for six years and sent an additional 300 "Trotskyists" to jail.

One year after he had arrived in Alma-Ata, Trotsky received an order banishing him from the Soviet Union. The president of Turkey, Kemal Pasha, granted him asylum, on condition that he stay on the isolated Turkish island of Prinkipo. Trotsky's friends, anxious to find him a home where he could work more easily, attempted to get him into Germany, but the Germans rejected the appeal. Once again Leon Trotsky was a man without a country. He left his homeland forever.

A Soviet hydroelectric station under construction in 1925. Lenin—and his successors—had an almost mystical belief in "electrification" and its power to modernize Russian agriculture. "Lenin's legacy," observes British historian Paul Johnson, "was a solidly built police state surrounded by economic ruins. But he went to eternity dreaming of electricity."

7

The Most Unwanted Man in the World

If Stalin believed that he had silenced Leon Trotsky for good, he underestimated his opponent's dedication. Other men in history had been exiled and had found themselves wandering around the world in search of a safe haven—often without success. Many hard men had been broken by banishment. But Leon Trotsky was to remain a fighter for the rest of his life.

For 22 days Trotsky and Natalya traveled the thousands of miles between Alma-Ata and Constantinople, the Turkish capital. Following their arrival, they were taken to Prinkipo and settled in the dilapidated villa that was to be their home for the next four years.

Trotsky immediately set about applying for admission to every democratic European and North American state. Germany, Great Britain, France, Austria, the Netherlands, Luxembourg, the United States, and Canada all quickly refused him. Though he knew that they would let him in if he renounced socialism, Trotsky continued to issue statements

Trotsky addresses Social Democratic students in Copenhagen, Denmark, in 1932. Determined to remain a thorn in the sides of those who, he believed, had betrayed the Russian Revolution, the exiled leader denounced Stalin in an endless stream of speeches, articles, and books.

Trotsky's Turkish exile provided ample time for both work and relaxation. During his four years (1929–33) on the island of Prinkipo, he wrote several influential books, including *The Permanent Revolution* and the autobiographical *My Life*.

Stalin (second from right, second row from bottom) at a 1930 party congress. Before banishing Trotsky in 1928, Stalin weakened his enemy's image by publicizing his old disputes with Lenin, downgrading his role in the revolution, and ordering his face removed from historical photographs. He then invented a crime called "Trotskyism."

reaffirming his belief in socialist revolution as the answer to mankind's problems and insisting that Stalin's regime was a monstrous aberration, an affront to the socialist ideal.

Adjusting to his situation, Trotsky began to devote ever-increasing amounts of energy and dedication to remorselessly wielding his oldest and most trusted weapon—the pen. When friends returned from visits to the island, their suitcases would be stuffed with his writings, which soon became widely available throughout Europe and North America. His talent for political analysis and forecasting received special recognition when, in 1930, he accurately predicted the triumph of fascism in Germany. In a pamphlet entitled "Germany, Key to the International Situation," Trotsky begged the German communists to look at their own recent gain of 1 million electoral votes in the context of the advance of 6 million votes gained by Adolf Hitler's violently anticommunist Nazi party. He urged the German communists to join with the Social Democrats to form a broader and more powerful anti-Nazi coalition.

Stalin undoubtedly longed to eliminate him, but at that point there were still too many people around who would have objected. Instead he cracked down on those who were helping Leon Trotsky distribute his writings. A leading official of the GPU (State Political Administration) named Blumkin, who visited Trotsky in 1929, was shot on Stalin's orders when he returned to the Soviet Union. The next desperate development was the official revocation of Trotsky and his family's Soviet citizenship, an enactment which made it treasonable for a Soviet citizen to contact them. Trotsky's response was to work even harder, to write even more.

In July 1933 friends in France managed to obtain visas for Trotsky and Natalya. Always afraid of Stalin's assassins, though, the family never stayed in one house for long. In 1934 they finally had one peaceful year alone in a cottage in the countryside, living under assumed names, but Trotsky could not bear being cut off from the political struggle. He felt,

Adolf Hitler (1889—1945) exhorts a crowd in the early 1930s. Although few heeded his warnings, Trotsky was among the first to predict that, if Hitler's Nazi party ever came to power in Germany, an invasion of the Soviet Union would be high on that country's list of foreign policy priorities.

Sergei Sedov Trotsky wrote Natalya and Trotsky a guarded, but clearly worried, letter in December 1934; they never heard from their son again. There was all too much reason, however, to believe he had been killed. "It is still possible," Trotsky wrote bitterly, "[for Stalin] to reward himself by striking at people close to me."

he said, as though he was living in a "moderately comfortable prison." All his clandestine connections with the Joint Opposition in the Soviet Union had been severed.

On December 1, 1934, Sergei Kirov, the Leningrad party boss and a member of Stalin's politburo (the party's political bureau), was assassinated. At first the government declared that the assassination had been orchestrated by White Guards, but then Stalin accused Trotsky, Zinoviev and Kamenev of complicity. Fifteen people were executed, and Zinoviev and Kamenev received long prison sentences.

Trotsky's diary entries for 1935 reveal the increasing misery and uncertainty of his situation. In April he wrote: "Alexandra Lvovna Sokolovskaya, my first wife, who was living in Leningrad with my grandchildren, has been deported to Siberia. . . . The letters from our younger son, Sergei, professor in the Institute of Technology, have stopped . . . from the age of twelve or so he turned his back on politics; he practiced gymnastics, loved the circus, and even wanted to become a circus performer; later he took up technical subjects, worked hard, and became a professor. If he has really been banished, there could be no political basis for it." Then, on June 1, it becomes apparent that the Trotsky family's fortunes have declined still further: "Sergei has been arrested; he is in prison; now it is no longer guesswork. . . . He was arrested, evidently, about the time our correspondence stopped. Almost half a year has elapsed since that time. . . . Poor boy. And my poor, poor Natasha." (Alexandra probably died in 1938. The fate of Nina's children is unknown.)

With the French Communist party strong and completely under the influence of Moscow, and with the open and savage destruction of everyone who opposed Stalin in the Soviet Union, it was becoming dangerous for Trotsky and Natalya to stay in France. In Norway, the Labor party had come to power and Trotsky once again asked for asylum. This time he received it.

On June 18, 1935, Trotsky, Natalya, and a secretary arrived at a secret place outside Oslo, Norway.

Somehow word of Trotsky's arrival had leaked out and Norwegian fascists were demonstrating there to demand Trotsky's deportation. Later, the Norwegian Communist party newspaper issued a statement making the same demand, but the Labor government held firm. A Labor party newspaper editorial vehemently asserted that Stalin had no right to "persecute and banish a man like Trotsky, whose name will stand beside Lenin's in the history of the Russian Revolution. Every democratic people must regard it as a duty of love to give him shelter."

Despite his indifferent health, Trotsky was able to complete *The Revolution Betrayed*—the book that increased his political influence more than any of his other works. It was a thorough analysis of the rise of Stalinism in the Soviet Union. Documenting the decline of Soviet democracy, it called upon the Soviet people to retain the socialist economic system and overthrow the Stalinist bureaucracy.

As translations of *The Revolution Betrayed* were read around the world, Stalin's reputation plummeted. Furthermore, the dictator's first Five Year Plan for the Soviet economy had failed miserably. Forcing the incorporation of private farms into state

"Mourners" following the bier of the assassinated Sergei Kirov include Stalin (center, behind carriage wheel). The true story of the 1934 murder of Kirov—who was shot in Leningrad's heavily guarded party headquarters—may never be known, but historians believe Stalin ordered the killing in order to justify initiating a purge of his enemies.

Trotsky and Natalya visit Copenhagen during a brief release from their Turkish exile in 1932. The couple—unwelcome in any European country—were greeted with hostility even in their host nation, Denmark, whose royal family was related to the murdered Russian tsar, and whose communists were supporters of Stalin.

collective farms had set Russian agriculture back 20 years. The kulaks, as owners of the largest farms, had burned their crops and killed their animals rather than submit to Stalin's orders. To distract the people from his own mistakes, Stalin embarked on a brutal purge of all whom he considered his opponents.

On August 19, 1936, Kamenev, Zinoviev, and 14 other leading Bolsheviks were brought to trial on charges of treason and terrorism. The official indictment stated that Trotsky and his son Lyova Sedov were at the center of the conspiracy and that the German secret police was directing the whole operation. The defendants were forced to make false confessions, found guilty, and executed. Trotsky and Lyova were tried in absentia and officially sentenced to death.

The Soviet government then instructed the Norwegians that if they failed to send Trotsky to the Soviet Union, the Soviets would no longer import Norway's main source of export earnings—herring.

The Norwegians refused to send Trotsky back to certain death, but they asked him to find another country willing to accept him.

Trotsky's friends and supporters everywhere were in a state of despair. How were they going to protect him? Was there anywhere in the world where their leader might live and work in peace? Then the famous Mexican artist Diego Rivera, himself a Trotskyist, urged Lazaro Cardenas, president of Mexico, to invite Trotsky and his entourage to their country. Rivera said that he and his wife, Frida Kahlo, would themselves house the refugees.

On January 9, 1937, Trotsky and Natalya arrived in Tampico, Mexico, aboard a Norwegian tanker. Meanwhile, 17 more prominent Soviet officials were arrested and accused of "Trotskyism." The Trotskys were taken to Rivera and Kahlo's charming house in Coyoacán, a suburb of Mexico City. The house, which had a lovely garden graced with ancient native South American statues and winding ornamental pathways, was surrounded by a high wall. Trotsky supporters and special Mexican police units stood guard 24 hours a day.

Fears for Trotsky's safety were not exaggerated. Another circus-like trial opened in Moscow on January 23, 1937. Again, innocent people were forced to confess to crimes against the Soviet state. As Trotsky and Natalya listened to the radio and read the newspapers, they felt, wrote Trotsky, that "insanity, absurdity, outrage, fraud, and blood were flooding us from all sides."

> *Bureaucratic autocracy must give place to Soviet democracy. A restoration of the right of criticism and genuine freedom of elections is the necessary condition for the further development of the country. This assumes a revival of freedom of Soviet parties, beginning with the Bolsheviks, and a renascence of the trade unions.*
> —LEON TROTSKY
> in his critique of Stalinism, *The Revolution Betrayed*, completed in 1936

A grim-faced row of judges presides over a 1930s "show trial." These legal mockeries featured elaborate false confessions, frequently obtained by torture, of conspiracies against the Soviet state. They usually resulted in mass executions. Trotsky, tried in absentia, was more than once condemned to death by such courts.

Trotsky and Natalya had no way of knowing that their youngest son, Sergei, was doomed. After his first arrest, he had been sentenced to five years in a Siberian prison camp. There he had met other Trotskyists, and, following the first Moscow trial, he had participated in their 132-day hunger strike. When an accident at the factory where Sergei worked caused the deaths of scores of workers, Stalin made Sergei the scapecoat. During the second trial, Sergei was sent to Moscow and charged with the "mass gassing of workers" under orders from his father.

Stalin hoped that, to save himself, Sergei would admit to anything. However, though physically ill from the hunger strike and the hard work conditions, Sergei would not break and sign a confession. The exact time and cause of his death were never discovered, but it was assumed that he was executed or fell ill and died, joining the unknown millions who perished in Stalin's labor camps.

Following the Moscow trials, Trotsky decided to organize an inquiry into these travesties of justice and, in particular, into the case against himself. Early in 1937 the British, French, Czechoslovak,

Arriving in Mexico in 1937, Trotsky and Natalya are welcomed by left-wing artist Diego Rivera (third from left; 1886–1957). Rivera, whose widely admired murals adorned many public places, had painted a heroic scene in New York City's Rockefeller Center in 1933. Outraged when he realized it contained figures resembling Lenin and Trotsky, millionaire Nelson Rockefeller had it removed.

and American committees for the Defense of Leon Trotsky decided to establish a Joint Commission of Inquiry. The purpose of the commission was to conduct an impartial investigation into the Soviet government's charges against Trotsky. A distinguished panel would come to Mexico and take Trotsky's testimony. Headed by the famous American philosopher and educator John Dewey, the commission was composed of prominent political figures from Europe and America. The members of the Joint Commission joined Dewey in Coyoacán to hold the historic hearing in April 1937.

In a series of 13 sessions, the first of which began on April 10, Trotsky presented evidence in his own defense. In its final report, the commission judged the Moscow trials to be an absolute sham, and found Trotsky innocent of Stalin's charges. News of the hearing attracted worldwide attention. Once again Joseph Stalin, head of state of a huge nation that had not ceased to fascinate the world since 1917, had suffered a blow to his prestige due to Leon Trotsky, a man without power, without a country.

Despite this moral victory, the growing horror of Stalin's purges took its toll on Trotsky and Natalya. They had given up hope that their son Sergei might still be alive. Trotsky described their situation in his autobiography: "We wandered about in our little tropical garden, surrounded by distant ghosts, each with a hole in his forehead."

Then temptation stepped into Trotsky's path, and he did not resist it. He had always been flirtatious with women, but Natalya had never seemed to take it seriously. At the age of 60, Trotsky still carried himself well. To take a break from the rigorous political schedule, the two couples, Diego Rivera and Frida Kahlo, Trotsky and Natalya, would go on occasional picnics.

Frida, an exotically beautiful woman of 29 and a fine artist in her own right, teasingly called Trotsky *El Viejo*, the Spanish version of the affectionate nickname that his American supporters had bestowed upon him—"the old man." Furthermore, she and Rivera had always conducted an open marriage, each tolerating the other's extramarital affairs. She

Determined to disprove Stalin's fantastic charges against him, Trotsky confers with his lawyer, Albert Goldman, before the 1937 hearings of the Joint Commission of Inquiry in Mexico City. His minutely detailed testimony persuaded the commission—and much of the rest of the world—that the Moscow trials had been "the greatest frame-up in history."

WORKERS OF THE WORLD UNITE IN THE IVTH INTERNATIONAL!

Trotsky was the centerpiece of Diego Rivera's 1938 mural advertising the Fourth International. Although he could not attend the Paris meeting, Trotsky wrote a pamphlet—"The Death Agony of Capitalism and the Tasks of the Fourth International"—that was adopted by the conference and is still the Fourth International's official program.

spoke to Trotsky in English, which the others could not understand, and made no secret of her interest in her distinguished houseguest. The flirtation soon became a love affair.

Natalya was then 55 years old and had been with Trotsky for 35 hard years. Far too dignified to create a scene, she wrote a discreet, pleading letter to her husband: "I saw myself in a mirror . . . and found I look much older. Our inner state has an enormous importance in our old age. . . ."

Trotsky's friends were afraid that his behavior would give rise to scandal; they knew the Stalinists would not hesitate to smear the reputation of "the old man" and they urged him to break off his romantic involvement. By midsummer, it was over, although the evidence suggests that it was Frida who ended the affair. In a note to friends, she had written: "I am very tired of the old man." Shortly after that, Natalya received a letter from her husband, in which he said: "I love you so much, Nata, my only one, my eternal, my faithful, my love and my victim!" Trotsky's infidelity could easily have wrecked his relationship with Natalya. However, tragedy came to reunite the couple.

Their son Lyova had been leading a terrifying existence as the number two target of the Soviet secret police. By the end of 1938, the Stalinist terror had claimed 3 million victims. Lyova had been working with one of Trotsky's aides, Rudolf Klement, to prepare the founding conference of the Fourth International—a new organization designed to bring together Trotsky's supporters all over the world and to counter Stalin's Third International. Soon afterward, Klement's mutilated body was found in the Seine River.

Lyova's one trusted friend was a young man named Mark Zborowski. Known in Trotskyist circles as Etienne, Zborowski was one of Lyova's coworkers on the Paris-based *Bulletin of the Opposition*. Lyova had been suffering appendicitis attacks for weeks, but he refused to go to a hospital.

The experience of my life has not only not destroyed my faith in the clear, bright future of mankind, but on the contrary, has given it an indestructible temper. This faith in reason, in truth, in human solidarity, I have preserved more fully and completely. It has become more mature but not less ardent.
—LEON TROTSKY
speaking in 1937

Less than a year after both he and Lyova had been condemned to death in a Moscow courtroom, Trotsky learned that his son was dead. "His mother and I," wrote the heartbroken exile, "are unable to believe that he is no more and weeping because it is impossible not to believe."

Natalya, Trotsky, and Seva in 1938. Although Seva, now 13, had not seen his grandfather for seven years, he had been raised almost to worship him. For his part, Trotsky was eager to explain to the boy the "ideas and purposes . . . for which our family . . . has suffered and is suffering so much."

Emissaries of the Soviet secret police are prowling in all countries of the Old and New World. They do not lack money. What does it mean to the ruling clique to spend twenty or fifty millions of dollars more or less, to sustain its authority and its power? These gentlemen buy human consciences like sacks of potatoes.

—LEON TROTSKY
speaking in 1937

He was sure he would be killed by a doctor or nurse bought off by Stalin's agents. Finally, Etienne persuaded him to enter a small clinic in Paris for surgery. Etienne and Jeanne Martin, Lyova's constant companion, visited him after the operation and he seemed fine. Then, on February 16, 1938, he was found wandering around the clinic's empty corridors, suffering from delirium and racked with pain. He died the next day. Etienne then took over the duties for which Lyova had been responsible.

Twenty years later, Etienne confessed that he himself had been Stalin's agent. When Lyova checked into the hospital Etienne had called the GPU.

About a month after Lyova's death, the third and most murderous Moscow trial commenced. Trotsky and former Comintern president Nikolai Bukharin were accused of having plotted to murder Lenin in 1918. Trotsky again stayed close to his radio, hearing reports of Bukharin's confessions, retractions, and retractions of retractions.

Even then, Trotsky neither resigned himself to keeping silent nor allowed himself to be overwhelmed by pessimism. He set to work writing a book analyzing Stalin, explaining the conditions that had made it possible for him to dominate the revolution. To the surprise of many of his followers, he continued to distinguish between Stalin's regime and the workers' state that the Russian Revolution had been intended to found. At the same time, Trotsky and his associates continued to prepare for the convening of the Fourth International. The founding conference took place near Paris on September 3, 1938, and was attended by 212 delegates from 11 countries.

Early in 1939, Rivera's intense antipathy toward Stalinism led him to declare his support for a right-wing candidate in Mexico rather than the candidate supported by Cardenas. Trotsky accused Rivera of "subjectivity" and made a public political break with the artist.

Supporters pooled their money to help Trotsky and Natalya buy their own house in Coyoacán. An alarm system was installed and guards from the ranks of the Fourth International maintained round-the-clock surveillance.

Natalya's emotional resilience was not of the same order as her husband's. After Lyova's death, she became increasingly silent and unsmiling—always a gracious hostess, but always sad. Anxious to make her happy, Trotsky asked Jeanne Martin to bring their only living grandchild, Seva, to Mexico. Jeanne and Lyova had taken care of Seva since the boy's mother, Zina—the daughter of Trotsky and Alexandra—had died some years before.

Jeanne was a member of a Trotskyist group in Paris that disagreed with Trotsky's analysis of the Soviet Union, and they threatened her with expulsion if she went with Seva to live with Trotsky and Natalya. Trotsky, albeit reluctantly, sued Jeanne and won custody of his grandson. Jeanne, however, rather than submit to the French court order, hid the child in an orphanage. In the summer of 1939 some old friends of Trotsky located Seva. In October they brought him to Coyoacán, much to the delight of Trotsky, who joyfully hugged and kissed his grandson. That same month, Trotsky's murderer arrived in Mexico.

Books explaining Trotsky's views are sold at New York City's Hippodrome, where 6,000 people had gathered in 1937 to hear Trotsky speak by telephone from Mexico. The telephone connection failed, but the speech was read to the crowd; in it, Trotsky denounced the trial at which he and his son Lyova had been condemned to death.

8

The Giant Killers

Stalin fumed while the exiled Leon Trotsky continued his political activity. Even the extermination of Trotsky's sons and grandchildren and most of his old friends had not stopped him. When the findings of the Dewey Commission were published and translations of *The Revolution Betrayed* appeared all over the world, Stalin's personal and political prestige sustained immense damage. The Soviet dictator now realized that only in death would Leon Trotsky keep silent.

Anxious to avoid blame for the assassination, Stalin turned the operation over to the Soviet security service. In 1938 the gruesome assignment was given to one of the most secret sections within the entire apparatus—the Division of Special Tasks, a crack group of spies and killers led by a man named Leonid Eitingon.

Though Trotsky would not allow suspicion and concern for his personal security to dominate his life, his loyal secretary-guards took the possibility of an assassination attempt very seriously. Visitors were not allowed anywhere near the house unless they had perfect credentials.

Trotsky knew that short of living in total isolation and abandoning his political struggle, there was no

Backed by Stalin (right) and Soviet Foreign Minister Vyacheslav Molotov (b. 1890), Nazi Foreign Minister Joachim von Ribbentrop (1893–1946) signs the Soviet-German nonaggression pact on August 23, 1939.

Stalin's obsession with Trotsky was matched by Trotsky's own preoccupation with his former colleague. The exiled Marxist talked and wrote almost ceaselessly about Stalin; his last book—uncompleted at his death—was *Stalin: An Appraisal of the Man and His Influence*, which even Trotsky's strongest supporters agreed was marred by his hatred for "the revolution's betrayer."

way that he could entirely discount the assassin's blade or bullet. Supporters from around the world who visited the house at Coyoacán commented on his relaxed attitude. Armed guards were always on duty both inside and outside the residence, but Trotsky scarcely seemed to notice. He spent his days in his study, an almost private wing of the building, researching, reading, and adding to his already impressive body of writing.

One of Stalin's agents who had attended the founding conference of the Fourth International in Paris in 1938 came up with a way to circumvent the tight security at Coyoacán. His plan hinged upon an American Trotskyist named Sylvia Agelof, who had served as a translator at the conference. Agelof was fluent in Russian, and she had spent time in Coyoacán helping Trotsky with his research. She was a plain-looking, apparently lonely woman in her late 20s. If someone could win her affection, she might unintentionally serve as a conduit to Trotsky.

The perfect candidate for that prospective infiltrator was close at hand. He was 27-year-old Ramon Mercader, the son of Eitingon's mistress, Caridad. He was attractive, charming, and able to speak several languages, including English. He introduced himself to Agelof as "Jacques Mornard," and claimed to be a graduate student of journalism at the Sorbonne University in Paris and the son of a Belgian diplomat. Mercader had stolen the identification papers of the real Jacques Mornard, who had no involvement in politics at all.

Mercader, alias Mornard, began a whirlwind courtship of Sylvia Agelof. Since he pretended that politics did not interest him, Agelof felt no immediate need to tell him about her involvement with the Trotskyists. When she did, he behaved as though he did not care; he was so in love with her he could be tolerant of any interest she pursued. He seemed to have a wallet that was always full, and, for the first time in her life, Agelof ate in expensive restaurants and received luxurious gifts. When she returned to New York in February 1939, her lover promised to join her soon.

Later that year, in September, World War II broke

Ramon Mercader, also known as Jacques Mornard and Frank Jacson, on his release from prison in 1960. Although Caridad, Mercader's mother, feared assassination by the GPU (Soviet secret police) after her son's imprisonment, knowledgeable Soviet-watchers doubted that the GPU would kill either mother or son, lest the survivor come forward with the true story of Trotsky's death.

out in Europe. In the troubled months before the commencement of hostilities, Stalin and his colleagues had made frantic attempts to fend off the possibility of a Nazi invasion of the USSR. Their efforts had been rewarded on August 23, 1939, when Germany and the Soviet Union signed a non-aggression pact. The Soviets did realize, however, that the treaty would probably not hold indefinitely.

But for the fact that, in their estimation, Trotsky's attitude made such a course of action impossible, Stalin and his clique might have considered shelving their plans to dispose of the exiled Oppositionist, so desperate was the European situation. "The Pen," however, continued to write prolifically, dashing off not only succinct and detailed criticisms of Stalin's pact with Hitler but also tracts condemning the new conflict as yet another fight between capitalists concerning spheres of influence.

In September 1939 Mercader arrived in New York. His forged Canadian passport bore the name of Frank Jacson. The GPU had decided that using the

Bullet holes in Trotsky and Natalya's bedroom offer silent testimony to the May 1940 machine-gun attack led by artist David Alfaro Siqueiros. Arrested, tried, and released on bail the following October, Siqueiros fled the country. When he returned to Mexico several years later, he resumed the life of a prominent and wealthy citizen.

name of a living person was too dangerous. Mercader pleased Agelof when he told her that he had changed his name because the Belgian military had drafted him and, like her, he was opposed to the war. He said influential friends had found him a job with a European trading company in Mexico.

After Mercader left for his "new job" in Mexico, he regularly wrote Agelof love letters urging her to join him. Before Christmas he sent her $3,000, and in January 1940 she flew to Mexico City.

Once he was with Agelof in Mexico, Mercader moved slowly and carefully. Through Agelof, he gained entry to the Trotsky house, made friends with Alfred and Marguerite Rosmer and Natalya, and chatted with the guards, especially a young American named Robert Sheldon Harte. He took care to give the people in Trotsky's entourage the impression that he was just a beginner where politics was concerned, and he refrained from asking to meet Leon Trotsky himself.

By the time Agelof flew back to New York in March, "Jacson" was known and well-liked at the Coyoacán fortress-house. Eitingon and Mercader's mother, Caridad, arrived in Mexico at the end of March to put to use the detailed information about Trotsky's house and habits that Mercader had supplied.

On May 24, 1940, Trotsky and Natalya were awakened at about 4:00 A.M. by bursts of machine-gun fire coming from within the grounds of the residence. Instinctively, they rolled out of bed to the narrow space on the floor between the bed and the wall. Their bed and the wall above their heads were sprayed with hundreds of bullets. In the next room, a terrified Seva yelled, "Grandpa!"

A fire bomb had set Seva's room ablaze. In the light of the fire, Natalya saw the shadow of a man in the hallway. The man loosed another round and ran off. With gunfire still audible in the distance, Trotsky and Natalya, both grazed by bullets but scarcely aware of their wounds, raced to Seva's smoke-filled room.

A moment later they found Seva, miraculously unharmed. He had hidden under his bed and then crawled out of the burning room. The whole household assembled in the courtyard. The Mexican sentries were found behind some shrubs, disarmed and tied up. The young American guard, Robert Sheldon Harte, had been kidnapped by the raiding party.

Almost immediately, Mexican Stalinists rushed to accuse Trotsky of trying to gain attention by hiring actors to machine-gun the house. Denied access to Mexican radio, Trotsky wrote angry articles refuting the charge. The theories of Colonel Sanchez Salazar, the Mexican police officer in charge of the investigation, also infuriated Trotsky. Salazar suggested that Harte was a GPU agent and had been in league with the would-be assassins. Indignantly, Trotsky told Salazar that his own son, Lyova, and seven of his former secretaries had been murdered by Stalin's agents. A month later, Harte's corpse was found miles away in a lime pit.

Through police informers, Salazar finally pieced much of the story together. The raid had been planned and staged by a vast network of Mexican Stalinists, many of whom were GPU agents. The leader of the assault had been the highly respected and celebrated Mexican painter, David Alfaro Siqueiros, a member of the Mexican Communist party and a bitter rival of Diego Rivera both artistically and politically. Uniformed as a Mexican army major, Siqueiros had led the raid on horseback.

It was not until the following October that Siqueiros was arrested and tried. Though he confessed to having helped organize the raid, Siqueiros stated that the purpose of the assault had been simply to protest Trotsky's presence in Mexico. "All enemies of the Communist party can expect similar treatment," he told the court. After the charges were reduced, he was released on bail and once again disappeared from Mexico.

Despite the lengthy investigation that followed the failed assassination attempt, none of the evidence pointed to Mercader as the source of the raiders' surprisingly detailed knowledge of the Trotskys' residence.

In the wake of this terrifyingly close call, Trotsky's family and friends urged him to go to the United States. They tried to convince him that supporters

A crude but potentially lethal bomb, discovered in Trotsky's house after the 1940 Siqueiros raid. Although he had been targeted for death by the Soviet leadership, and the socialist dream had degenerated severely, Trotsky continued to defend the Soviet Union.

could slip him into the country and hide him. Trotsky, realizing that such a course of action would condemn him to silence, rejected their suggestions. He declared that he would not spend whatever time he had left fleeing death. Reluctantly, however, he did agree to the installation of electronic warning devices at the gates, bombproofing of the floors and walls of his study, the fitting of steel doors and shutters, and the raising of the height of the wall around the villa's compound. When he viewed the completed renovation, he sighed and told Natalya, "This is not a home; it is a medieval prison." Having never allowed his guards, despite their urging, to search visiting friends, Trotsky still declined to change his policy. The decision was to prove fatal.

Stalin could not stand the fact that tiny Trotskyist Fourth International groups were challenging communist parties all over the world. As Trotsky's political outpourings continued, Stalin's rage at the fresh damage the bungled assassination attempt had done to his reputation became uncontrollable. Orders were given that the assignment be completed, and Eitingon decided that this time there should be a single assassin, someone who would probably be shot by the guards after he had killed Trotsky, and who would therefore remain silent for-

A Mexican policeman displays the ice axe with which Ramon Mercader murdered Trotsky. When Trotsky's guards caught Mercader, he was holding a .45 pistol; he had also carried a 14-inch dagger. Trotsky had two guns of his own in his study but never had the chance to defend himself.

Bloodstains and overturned furniture mark the scene of Trotsky's doomed struggle for his life. Near death, Trotsky told Natalya, "You know, in there, I sensed . . . I understood what he wanted to do . . . He wanted to strike me once more . . . but I didn't let him. . . . "

ever. Ramon Mercader, alias Frank Jacson, who had easy access to the house, was the logical choice. He would now have to get close to "the old man."

"Jacson" visited the house several times, bringing toys for Seva and pretending that he was becoming increasingly interested in Trotskyist politics.

In August 1940 "Jacson" asked one of the secretaries if Trotsky would read an article he had written. The secretary thought little of "Jacson"'s political abilities and advised Trotsky not to waste his time, but Trotsky agreed to meet with him.

It may have been a dress rehearsal for the murder or perhaps "Jacson" lost his nerve, but on August 17, 1940, in Trotsky's study, he stood slightly behind Trotsky, with a coat slung over his arm. Trotsky remarked to Natalya that "Sylvia's young man" seemed to be tense and neurotic and that his article was barely coherent.

In the late afternoon of the next day, "Jacson" appeared at the house again. He asked Natalya for a glass of water, and she noticed that his hands were shaking. It was a hot day, but he was still carrying his coat on his arm. Trotsky was nearby, feeding his rabbits, and "Jacson" strolled over to him and showed him a freshly typed and edited manuscript. Humbly, he asked Trotsky if he would take another look at it.

Once he has done with the anarchic forces of his own society, man will set to work on himself. Mankind will regard itself as raw material, or at best as a physical and psychic semi-finished product. Socialism will mean a leap from the realm of necessity into the realm of freedom in this sense also, that the man of today, with all his contradictions and lack of harmony, will open the road for a new and happier race.
—LEON TROTSKY
in his last public speech,
delivered in Copenhagen
in 1932

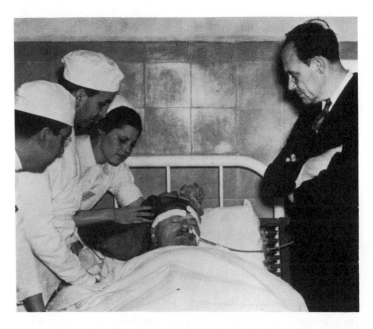

Doctors and nurses watch helplessly as Trotsky's life ebbs. Natalya remained by his side during the 22 hours between surgery and death. "The features of his face," she later wrote, "retained their purity and pride. It seemed that any moment now he might still straighten up and become his own master again."

Again "Jacson" stood behind Trotsky, who scanned the article for nearly 10 minutes. Then, in a swift movement, "Jacson" pulled from under his coat a mountaineer's ice axe, a short-handled instrument with one sharp edge and one hammer claw. He later described to a prison psychiatrist what he had done next: "I . . . took it in my fist, and closing my eyes, gave him a tremendous blow on the head. . . . The man screamed in such a way that I will never forget as long as I live. I saw Trotsky get up like a madman. He threw himself at me and hit my hand. Then I pushed him, so that he fell to the floor. He lifted himself as best he could and then, running or stumbling . . . he got out of the house."

Natalya had raced to the study when she heard the commotion. She threw her arms around Trotsky as he collapsed while saying, "Jacson." She knelt beside him, straining to hear his fading voice. "Natalya, I love you," he whispered. "Seva must be taken away from all this."

Although he had received a deep wound in his brain, Trotsky fought against losing consciousness. From the study, he and Natalya could hear the guards screaming at "Jacson," beating him mercilessly in their rage. Trotsky whispered to Natalya,

"Tell the boys not to kill him. He must talk." Even near death he was outthinking Stalin.

Trotsky was rushed to the hospital, where immediate surgery was ordered. He joked with Natalya about his "haircut" and dictated a message to his followers around the world: "I am close to death from the blow of a political assassin. . . . Please say to our friends . . . I am sure . . . of the victory . . . of the Fourth International. . . . Go forward."

Surgery was performed, but the wound was too deep. That evening, as Natalya sat at the foot of his bed, her husband gasped his last words: "I feel in my heart that this time they have succeeded." He lapsed into a coma and never regained consciousness. On the evening of the following day, August 21, 1940, Leon Trotsky died.

Mercader, though willing to divulge the details of his crime, refused to give his real name or explain his motives. (Years later, when his fingerprints were checked out in Spain, his true identity was discovered and the truth began to emerge.) In the Soviet

The sights and sounds of past violence recalled only by a crumbling gun turret, Trotsky's garden provides a peaceful setting for one of his great-granddaughters in 1970. Seva, his wife, and three daughters lived in his grandfather's house for three decades after the old revolutionary was murdered.

Union, the official Communist party newspaper, *Pravda*, announced that Trotsky had been killed by a disillusioned follower. Stalin, however, gave Caridad, Ramon Mercader's mother, a medal for herself and one to hold for her son.

In 1960, after 20 years in jail, Mercader, still refusing to admit either his own name or those of the men who had issued his orders, was released and taken to the Czech embassy. Thereafter, he disappeared into total obscurity.

On the day after Trotsky's death an eight-mile long crowd followed the pallbearers through the streets of Mexico City. Over the next five days, 300,000 people entered the funeral home and filed past the coffin to look at Leon Trotsky. As he had requested, his ashes were placed beneath a plot of cactus in the garden at Coyoacán. A red flag and a stone monument carved with a hammer and sickle, the symbol of the union between workers and peasants, were erected nearby.

Trotsky's influence lived on long after his own death and long after that of Stalin, who died in 1953. In the late 1960s, for example, Trotsky's followers among students in the United States, France, Germany, Britain, and Mexico were influential in the movements against the Vietnam War.

After Trotsky's death, Natalya continued to live in Coyoacán with Seva. In 1956 she made a request to the Soviet government that Trotsky, Lyova, and other victims of the Moscow trials be rehabilitated. Despite the fact that in that same year Nikita Khrushchev, who was then first secretary of the Communist party of the Soviet Union, had revealed some of the horrors of the Stalin period and rehabilitated many executed Bolsheviks, he and his colleagues in the party hierarchy refused to extend the same privilege to Trotsky.

Natalya then went to stay with friends in Paris, where she died, at age 79, in 1962. Her ashes were brought to Coyoacán and placed under the cactus plants beside the ashes of Leon Trotsky.

Over the years thousands of people visited the study of "the old man" who, on a bitterly cold night in October 1917, had issued the order to capture

The writings of this extraordinary man are likely to survive, and the example of his energy and heroism likely to grip the imagination of generations to come. Trotsky embodied the modern historical crisis with an intensity of consciousness and a gift for dramatic response which few of his contemporaries could match: he tried, on his own terms, to be equal to his time. In his power and his fall, Leon Trotsky is one of the titans of our century.

—IRVING HOWE

the Winter Palace; who had led armies across the length and breadth of Russia to save the Bolshevik revolution; who had transformed, through the sheer force of his oratory and willpower, ordinary working men and women into ardent revolutionaries; who wrote books that to this day line the shelves of libraries all over the world; who was gifted with a personality—dedicated, brilliant, contradictory—that would continue to intrigue students of politics for generations.

On February 27, 1940, just months before the assassin's blow struck him down, the 60-year-old Trotsky had written: "My faith in the Communist future of mankind is not less ardent, indeed it is firmer today, than it was in the days of my youth." He continued: "Natalya has just come up to the window from the courtyard and opened it wider so that the air may enter more freely into my room. I can see the bright green strip of grass beneath the wall, and the clear blue sky above the wall, and sunlight everywhere. Life is beautiful. Let the future generations cleanse it of all evil, oppression, and violence and enjoy it to the full."

A silent, grieving crowd accompanies Trotsky's casket through Mexico City on August 22, 1940. Six months earlier, he had composed his will, which included the statement: "If I were to begin all over again . . . the course of my life would remain unchanged. I shall die a proletarian revolutionary. . . ."

Further Reading

Archer, Jules. *Trotsky: World Revolutionary.* New York: Julian Messner, 1973.

Deutscher, Isaac. *The Prophet Armed: Trotsky, 1879–1921.* New York: Oxford University Press, 1954.

———. *The Prophet Unarmed: Trotsky, 1921–1929.* New York: Oxford University Press, 1959.

———. *The Prophet Outcast: Trotsky, 1929–1940.* New York: Oxford University Press, 1963.

Herrera, Hayden. *A Biography of Frida Kahlo.* New York: Harper & Row Publishers, Inc., 1983.

Howe, Irving, ed. *The Basic Writings of Trotsky.* New York: Random House, Inc., 1963.

Payne, Robert. *The Life and Death of Leon Trotsky.* New York: McGraw-Hill Book Co., 1977.

Segal, Ronald. *Leon Trotsky.* New York: Pantheon Books, 1979.

Serge, Victor, and Natalia Sedova Trotsky. *The Life and Death of Leon Trotsky.* New York: Basic Books, Inc., 1975.

Trotsky, Leon. *My Life.* New York: Pathfinder Press, 1970.

Trotsky, Leon. *The Revolution Betrayed.* Garden City, New York: Doubleday & Co., Inc., 1937.

Wolfe, Bertram D. *Three Who Made a Revolution.* New York: Dell Publishing Co., Inc., 1964.

Wyndham, Francis, and David King. *Trotsky: A Documentary.* New York: Praeger Publishers, 1972.

Chronology

Oct. 26, 1879	Born Lev Davidovich Bronstein, in Yanovka, Russia
1889–96	Attends school in Odessa
Jan. 27, 1898	Arrested for involvement in revolutionary activities
1898–1900	Period of imprisonment in several Russian jails
1900	Marries Alexandra Lvovna Sokolovskaya
	Exiled to Siberia
Oct. 1902	Escapes from Siberia and travels to London to work with Lenin and other expatriate Russian revolutionaries
Nov. 1902	Meets Natalya Sedova, who becomes his mistress and constant companion
July–Aug. 1903	Procedural disputes result in division of All-Russian Social-Democratic Labor party into two competitive factions—Lenin's "hard left" Bolsheviks and Martov's "moderate" Mensheviks
1905	Trotsky returns to Russia in wake of workers' uprising in St. Petersburg, assumes leading role, and serves as chairman of St. Petersburg soviet
1906–17	Second period of imprisonment and exile
March 2, 1917	Provisional Government takes power following abdication of Tsar Nicholas II
Oct. 25, 1917	Bolsheviks, led by Trotsky and Lenin, seize power from Provisional Government and declare Russia a communist state
March 3, 1918	Signs separate peace with Germany at Brest-Litovsk, ceding large areas of Russian territory
1918–21	Serves as people's commissar for war
1923	Feud between Trotsky and Stalin develops
Jan. 21, 1924	Lenin dies
May 1924	Trotsky censured by central committee of Russian Communist party (Bolsheviks) and removed as people's commissar for war
Dec. 1925	Prohibited from making speeches by central committee
Jan. 1929	Banished by Stalin from the Soviet Union
1929–33	Period of exile in Turkey
1933–35	Period of exile in France
1935–37	Period of exile in Norway
Aug. 1936	Kamenev, Zinoviev and 14 other leading Bolsheviks stand trial on fabricated charges of treason and terrorism
Jan. 9, 1937	Trotsky arrives in Mexico
Aug. 21, 1940	Dies, aged 60, in Mexico City, of head wounds inflicted by Stalin's agent Ramon Mercader

Index

Hedda Garza lives in upstate New York, where she works as a political consultant for the State University of New York, and as a freelance writer, editor, indexer, and lecturer. Her articles have appeared in several national magazines and her *Watergate Investigation Index* won the best academic book award from *Choice* magazine.

Arthur M. Schlesinger, jr., taught history at Harvard for many years and is currently Albert Schweitzer Professor of the Humanities at City University of New York. He is the author of numerous highly praised works in American history and has twice been awarded the Pulitzer Prize. He served in the White House as special assistant to presidents Kennedy and Johnson.